A Practical Guide to Community Ministry

A Practical Guide

Guide

to Community Ministry

Ministry

A. David Bos

Westminster/John Knox Press
Louisville, Kentucky

Book design by Laura Lee

Cover design by Laura Lee

First edition

Published by Westminster/John Knox Press
Louisville, Kentucky

This book is printed on acid-free paper that meets the American National Standards Institute Z39.48 standard. ∞

PRINTED IN THE UNITED STATES OF AMERICA
9 8 7 6 5 4 3 2 1

Library of Congress Cataloging-in-Publication Data

Bos, A. David.
   A practical guide to community ministry / A. David Bos. — 1st ed.
      p.   cm.
   Includes bibliographical references.
   ISBN 0-664-25405-5 (pbk. : alk. paper)

   1. Church work.   2. Pastoral theology.   3. Interdenominational cooperation.   I. Title.
BV4400.B64   1993
253—dc20   93-10749

To my mother and father, Alvin D. and Eunice Hyma Bos, whose devotion to their respective callings in their particular place, Holland, Michigan, inspired me to do the work of community ministry.

Contents

Acknowledgments

I AM DEEPLY INDEBTED to The Ministries of Suffolk County, Long Island, New York, and St. Matthews Area Ministries of Louisville, Kentucky, which I have served as executive director and which have encouraged my writing and research on the subject of community ministry. The latter allowed me a ten-month leave of absence for the purpose of writing this book. A grant from the Lilly Endowment and a stipend from the Reformed Church of France, together with housing provided by the Quissac/Sauve parish, made this writing and research financially possible.

I am also grateful to the executive directors of community ministries in Louisville and Jefferson County, Kentucky, and to those of the steering committee of the national Interfaith Community Ministries Network who have read and commented on parts of the manuscript.

My wife, Johanna, and son, Martin, graciously accommodated their lives to the writing of this book and supported and encouraged me through the years when it was taking shape.

Preface

IN THE LATE 1960s faith communities in the United States engaged in wide-ranging experimentation that was meant to impact the social fabric. Experiments were found from local to worldwide levels and ranged from innovation in worship to recreation. New ecumenical and interfaith ministries began to spring up, some of which were referred to as "experimental ministries."

For the most part the new ministries were not connected to each other and did not view themselves as part of a larger movement. But in retrospect there were several spontaneous and simultaneous explosions of ecumenical/interfaith energy in urban neighborhoods, small towns, rural counties, recreational areas, industrial sites, and primary market areas of enclosed shopping malls. Each project was unique, but each was also more a part of a larger development than their founders knew.

I was there at one of the first of those outbursts of energy. My denomination had engaged me to conduct a year's exploration into the question of what the strategy of the denomination should be in a particular area of Long Island. In the spirit of the times, this was to have been an open-ended exploration. Almost no limits were set as to what ideas could be entertained.

Recommendations were sought from an ecumenical and interfaith group of twelve who felt that they had something at stake in the denomination's decision. Their proposal to serve the area through an ecumenical/interfaith community ministry was approved. Thus, The Ministries of Suffolk County, one of the first community ministries, was born. That was in the spring of 1967. By 1974, we were receiving letters and delegations from all around the United States and beyond (including Canada and Australia), inquiring about this form of ministry.

In 1977 I came to St. Matthews Area Ministries (St. MAM) in Louisville, Kentucky. I was surprised to find several such ministries in that city. Unknowingly I had come to one of the capital cities of the movement. By 1981, the community ministries of Louisville began to discuss supporting each other through a conference. What started out as a local project quickly developed into one of regional interest, and people came to it from as far afield as Tulsa, Oklahoma, and Washington, D.C. We soon saw that we were a part of a movement that was nationwide.

By the time of a subsequent (and truly national) consultation in 1988, there seemed to be a need for a communications network through which the ministries could support and inform each other. I was asked to chair a steering committee that was mandated by the conference to form an Interfaith Community Ministries Network—as we eventually called ourselves.

A few years ago I began to write down my thoughts about these events. It seemed to me that there were some lessons to draw from the movement's first twenty years. Such is the task that I have set for myself in this book, which does not pretend to be a theoretical or biblical/theological treatment of social ministry. I would like it to serve as a practical guide for those congregations and parishes that would engage each other to minister in and with their several communities. Also, I hope that my contribution will stimulate others to bring disagreements, additional issues, and information to light.

In concept, community ministry is one thing, though individual community ministries are as unique as their immediate environment, whether they are located in rural counties, small towns, old or new suburbs, or urban neighborhoods. We are co-participants in a significant movement, experiencing the same tensions and problems, the same sense of absolute uniqueness based on the unique characteristics of our locales, and the same exhilaration that comes from a ministry that is truly local, social, and ecumenical/interfaith.

Introduction:
What Is Community Ministry?

THE TERM COMMUNITY MINISTRY is some-
times used to embrace all the means available to a congregation in coming to terms with its immediate social context. But
the community ministry that I have in mind refers to a particular
way of ministering to society in which congregations of more
than one denomination and of a particular locality (neighborhood, small town, rural county) agree to pool their resources.

Used in this way, the term *social ministry* refers to a dimension
of the total ministry of any religious body—the dimension in
which it responds to its context as best it can in faith, hope, and
love. In this book we speak of a local social ministry, or how a
congregation responds in faith, hope, and love to the neighborhood, town, or rural county that comprises its immediate context.

What exactly do we mean by the term *local*? The World Council of Churches refers to nationally organized church bodies as
"local churches"—a usage that is not supported by English dic-
tionaries. *Local* refers to the immediate environs where people
live and work. International and national organizations use the
word to indicate an entity that is relatively more local than the
purview of their organization. In community ministry we know
that *local* cannot be relativized so easily. As a practical matter,
we are speaking of a population of twenty to fifty thousand inhabitants (whether in a few city blocks or several rural counties). Community ministries that embrace larger areas tend to
become umbrella organizations requiring subdivisions in order

to sustain the claim of being responsive to people where they live and work. Areas of under about twenty thousand inhabitants find it difficult to support a community ministry that is staffed and accessible on a full-time basis. The phrase "at the most local level possible," which appeared in a paper written several years ago by Nathan van der Werf for the National Council of Churches,[1] is a fortunate one because it tends to push the definition of *local* to where people live out their daily lives. In this book I respond to the question: How does a congregation best serve its own neighborhood? That is, how does a congregation minister in and with its own community?

Thus community ministry, as in "the community ministry movement," possesses three vital and energizing characteristics: It is congregation-based and very local, covering as small an area as is practicable. It is a social ministry that sees the issues through the prism of its own community. It is ecumenical, interfaith, or both.

1   Ministry at the Most Local Level Possible

Several Congregations, One Parish

IT IS WORTH NOTING that one of the precursors of the community ministry movement was called the East Harlem Protestant Parish. By *parish* one understands a local community: its population, institutions, history, and problems for which people of faith take genuine responsibility. The word *parish* points to one's immediate area as a focus for mission—a concept generally less familiar to Protestants than to Catholics. This word allows Protestant congregations in particular to view the claims of the surrounding community as legitimate. If a congregation were presented with a charge upon joining a community ministry, it might read like this:

> Your membership in the community ministry stands for a new level of commitment by your congregation to the immediate community. Through this ministry you say that you are taking the community's needs seriously and that you will invest leadership, facilities, and funds on a cooperative basis in order to define and respond to those needs, that your support of missions in other places will not excuse you from the one in your own front yard, and that you have a social and ecumenical/interfaith ministry that is local.

Basic Implications of
Congregation-Based Ministry

A community ministry in St. Louis calls itself simply the Five Church Association. This name describes the reality of most community ministries: They have no standing apart from their constituent congregations. Although some ministries admit organizations other than congregations, the relationship to congregations is at the heart of their identity and sets community ministry apart from other forms of ecumenical/interfaith or social ministry.

The umbilical relationship between a congregation and its community ministry has several implications that are important for understanding our movement. Chief among these is that congregations may view the community ministry as an integral part of their mission. They may make claims upon it that they could not or would not make upon other organizations in which they participate.

The leadership of the ministry will be drawn from the leadership of the member congregations. Therefore it will minister to its community as conservatively or progressively as the member congregations taken as a whole. Yet as congregations grow in their understanding of social responsibility and in willingness to consider various options, the community ministry experiences greater freedom of action. For example, the mere mention of the word *housing* in a public address by a new staff member of a community ministry brought an anonymous letter purporting to represent the views of eleven churchwomen. Addressed to the mayor, it accused the staff member of wanting to foist low-income housing on the community. How vulnerable and limited a local ministry can be when it touches the exposed nerves of its neighborhood or parish! But once a ministry has the support of its churches on a particular issue, its impact in the community is incalculable.

Ten years later in that same community a house rented by an interracial couple was vandalized. At the suggestion of one community ministry board member, several board members met during Holy Week—only days after the attack. The group issued a statement deploring the incident and called for a public effort toward rectification, prosecution of the perpetrators, and support for a newly formed housing coalition that was addressing fair housing and housing problems on a broad scale. This statement was placed in the foyers of all the churches that could get organized quickly with signature sheets and collection plates. The result was that on Easter Sunday over fifteen hundred signatures were collected, together with the funds to publish them on a full-page "Easter Greeting" in the local weekly. In addition, several hundred dollars were collected for repairs on the house, the mayor went on record as being opposed to any form of housing discrimination, and the community ministry became a founding member of the new housing coalition. It took ten years and an act of vandalism before that ministry could begin to deal with the housing issue. Such is the sensitivity of a community ministry to the readiness of its congregations.

Community ministry counteracts the notion that the church is a voluntary association, unrelated specifically to a neighborhood or community, and it encourages a sense of pastoral responsibility for the immediate social context. It furthers the advocacy of indigenous cultural, social, economic, and political patterns against those imposed from outside. It embraces some positive values of localism: that development should not proceed at the expense of a sense of community; that strong local communities are the best way of assuring a healthy metropolis or region; that self-determination at the local level is the best way of promoting participation at other levels; and that decentralization of the control of resources makes for more accountability and less waste. All of these points may be restated in terms of intra-ecclesiastical and ecumenical relations as "values" of community ministry. Nevertheless, community ministry may be regarded as ponderous by those who see the need for rapid action to combat a particular form of social injustice.

A Local Ecumenical and Social Ministry— Contradictions in Terms?

During an interview, one director of a community ministry expressed frustration when I used the words *local ecumenism* because she feared that the phrase was a contradiction in terms.

First, she was not sure that anything as local as a community ministry could be ecumenical in the sense of embracing the whole world. Second, she feared that when churches came together under the banner of "cooperation for service" (as they often do in community ministry) it tended to excuse them from working for greater unity. As she put it, "They really don't give up anything for each other." The issues that she raises are not just abstractions. Millions of church dollars and tens of millions of other dollars are going into community ministry each year now. Are these great and growing resources supporting a movement that is irrelevant to the cause of unity among Christians and antipathetic toward global issues? Certainly there is a side to the ideology of localism that stresses local control without reference to its effect on the larger society. It finds its ecclesiastical expression in utter distrust of denominational or ecumenical structures beyond the local level. Thus it does happen that a congregation, unwilling to give more than lip service to denominational ties (or to the ecumenical ties of the denomination), is willing to participate in a community ministry provided the frame of reference remains strictly local. Then, too, ministry at the most local level possible does run the risk of reinforcing exclusivist and isolationist attitudes. It is understandable therefore that community ministry might seem in the view of denominational offices to be a diversion from the larger, "real" issues. To them it might seem a bit contrived to argue that a large suburban congregation's discovery of its own local social ministry will make it more empathetic to the ministries of other, less well-off congregations—although experience has proven this to be the case. At times it must seem preferable that such a congregation bypass its own neighborhood in allocating social ministry resources.

Stan Esterle, executive director of Highlands Community Ministries in Louisville for over twenty years, points out one problem: "Community ministry usually functions through consensus rather than through majority votes precisely because the ties that bind are so fragile. But consensus is difficult to achieve on any given issue."[2] Quite often it is a struggle to shape a social ministry that goes beyond direct service. Esterle says the toughest part of working with the same congregations over many years has been "to persuade them to broaden the scope of their connections to each other," whether in the field of social ministry or in the pursuit of ecumenical/interfaith goals.[3]

Modest Agendas

Community ministry rarely begins with specific commitments to ecumenical/interfaith relations or to handed-down, social justice priorities. The word *ecumenical* means "pertaining to the whole inhabited world." In churches, the word is used to indicate a commitment to the unity of Christians worldwide and, by extension, in every place. But joining a community ministry may not imply even a minimal commitment to other congregations—much less to the traditions with which those congregations are associated—or to the ecumenical/interfaith agenda of those traditions. The only commitment that one can count on is that of doing some form of social ministry cooperatively in the local community. Thus there is a certain burden of proof that rests with the community ministry movement. What kind of cooperative relationships and social ministry does it finally stand for?

A Vision of Transcendent Localism

The question with which we began (How does a congregation minister in and with its own community?) now becomes: How does a congregation participate in wider circles of ecumenical/interfaith and social ministry through its work in and with the local community?

If it is true that we cannot speak of an environmental or social issue that is strictly local, it is just as true that these issues have their ramifications in each locality. The challenge for a cluster of congregations is to dig deeply into and understand the problems of its immediate area. Then any involvement beyond the local will carry the mark of authenticity because it will have been grounded locally. For example, the DOVE ministries of Decatur, Illinois, responded to a group of women meeting at the local "Y" and sponsored their educational project on domestic violence. Eventually DOVE became a major educational resource on the subject through seminars it conducted for area-wide denominational groupings. Its executive director received invitations from around the country to speak on the subject. The Illinois Conference of Churches asked that ministry to consider providing resources for a statewide ministry on family violence.

At the North Dallas Shared Ministries, volunteers found that many who were requesting emergency food supplies were unaware of their eligibility for food stamps. After repeated attempts to get food stamp centers to publicize the eligibility requirements, a volunteer took it upon himself to develop a "food stamp rights" flier. This flier proved so popular that it eventually appeared in almost all the food stamp offices in greater Dallas. On the street it became the acknowledged best source of information on the program.

These illustrations show how the phrase "Think globally; act locally," a peace movement slogan that reflects an awakening to the local dimension, may be experienced again in community ministry. The "act locally" part of the equation is now in place in many communities, just waiting to be informed by the "think globally" part.

Community ministry is fertile ground for anyone who is skilled in thinking ecumenically and globally and for whom "local" is an expandable context leading to overarching concerns. Ask the questions: Who is financing the new development that borders on several backyards? What decisions are being made in that bank or insurance company boardroom a thousand miles away that affect the future of the community? Whence come the town's polluted air and acid rain? What would be the impact of a regional environmental disaster on the neighborhood?

Although it is a continuous, difficult struggle to move through the local to deeper levels of ecumenical/interfaith and social ministry, it takes only the personal involvement of one member of one congregation, one recipient of services, one volunteer or noted local personage to establish the legitimacy of an issue. St. Matthews Area Ministries (St. MAM) of Louisville, Kentucky—prompted by the fact that the local Catholic bishop had been

involved in drafting a pastoral letter on nuclear weapons—
found reason enough to hold a series of open forums on the
subject in which the bishop graciously participated.

Community ministries can model on a congregational scale
the complementary relationship between ecumenism and social
justice. Stan Esterle (whose frustrations we have already noted)
can point to some notable achievements that include the
founding of several neighborhood organizations and a board
that coordinates them, an advocacy-oriented community organization, a community development corporation, and several innovative social ministry programs. Moreover, this ministry
developed a covenant through which member congregations
bind themselves to each other and to an agenda that combines
the ecumenical and the social. The churches of this ministry approved a common baptismal certificate, which every person in
those churches receives upon their baptism. It symbolizes en-
trance into a local Christian community that transcends denominational boundaries. These remarkable results show that it is
possible for a community ministry to become a model expression of ecumenism and social justice ministry combined.

I remember as a child being fascinated and amused by the
notion that in order to get to the other side of the world (China,
perhaps) one had only to dig straight down from the spot
where one was standing—if only one dug deeply enough! The
truth is, if a community ministry digs deeply enough into its local situation, its impact will be felt far beyond that area—perhaps to the other side of the world! Yes, in doing community
ministry, we will discover myriad points of correspondence with
other communities, but we can transcend the local community
only by working in and through it.

2 Pastoral Action:
Social Ministry as a Form of
Pastoral Care

WHEN WE GROUND SOCIAL MINISTRY in the local community, we recognize it as both an expression and an expansion of pastoral care. As a pastoral expression, social ministry may be inferred from the key words *parish* and *ministry*. *Parish* implies worshiping communities at the center, generating mutual care that overflows into the community at large. *Ministry* embraces a variety of functions, all of which are related and are expressions of the whole. This linkage is experienced in the community ministries movement above all by the connection between pastoral care and social ministry. We come to understand, for example, that the pastoral needs of an individual have a social dimension and that their resolution may require social action.

As an expansion of pastoral care, community ministry restores the capability of churches to care for the community as a whole. Our focus on the most local level possible makes it relatively easy to see the individual's problem as a problem of the community. One person's need might lead in any number of directions. Opening a child-care center has led to support for child-care legislation. Responding to chemical dependency and codependency problems has led to discussions on the addictive society. Operating a youth center has lead to advocating improvements in the juvenile justice system. Ongoing programs of community ministry constitute a framework for uncovering systemic problems and advocating solutions. It is simply incorrect and inaccurate to describe community ministries as "service ministries," just as it would be incorrect to describe social ministry in general this way. Social service, with its emphasis on helping the individual, is only part of a larger picture that includes community organization, community development, advocacies of various kinds, direct action, and other forms of social ministry, all of which may be found within community ministry under the rubric of "caring for the community."

The more local and ecumenical the organization, the closer the relationship between social ministry and pastoral care. Ministry becomes more holistic around these two poles, while each acquires more legitimacy in the process. One illustration of the above is the social work profession's reclaiming of its historic link to social ministry. Barbara Solomon, professor at the University of Southern California, Los Angeles, has suggested that counseling agencies place clinical social workers in inner-city churches.[4]

Solomon cites research showing that in a pilot project, individuals and families who had never sought services from traditional counseling agencies came to the church-based programs. Scores of others came who had been to traditional agencies and dropped out due to feelings of frustration and hopelessness engendered by what was perceived to be insensitivity on the part of the agencies. The church-based delivery system was uniquely capable of helping people appreciate their own strengths and take control of their lives. Solomon posits a relationship between skilled counseling and community empowerment: "The prevention of distress will inevitably require that we counter the effects of the eroding community. It is the cohesive community that is perhaps the greatest hope for a more functional society in which all of us are empowered to reach our potential as human beings."[5]

Thus the rise to prominence of the clinical social worker, a development some see as a symptom of social work in bondage to individualistic values, becomes a potential force for building community when put in the context of local church cooperation. When the focus is local and the context is ecumenical, we are most likely to engage in the kind of social ministry that Dieter Hessel has called "multi-mode"[6]—one that utilizes all the modalities and resources of religious life in a given locality for the sake of building up the community and the individuals in it. In most localities the marriage of pastoral care and social action centers on efforts to improve the quality of life so that people have a sense of actually living in a community. Joe Holland, social critic and regular contributor to the *National Catholic Reporter*, has coined the term "pastoral action," by which he means action toward social justice based upon pastoral care motivations and concerns: "The hunger for community is perhaps one of the most important pastoral indicators in a society marked by rootlessness, fragmentation, and spiritual sterility.[7]

Whether a community ministry chooses the perspective of a Barbara Solomon or a Joe Holland, it finds itself uniquely placed to view the community as a whole, and therefore to care for the community as a whole.

Assessing the Need

Let us acknowledge at the outset that community ministry responds to two sets of needs: the needs of the community and the needs of the churches that make up the membership of the ministry. Some portion of the program is determined by the need to build cooperative relationships between the churches so that there might be an effective cooperative response to the needs of the community. The programs developed specially for the church constituency may or may not coincide with community needs. For example, a church youth group would like to undertake a community service project. The community ministry attempts to match the request to some need in the community. The same group may ask for an educational program about the work of the ministry, for a program on the ecumenical movement, or for coordinated visits to other churches for the purpose of learning more about them. Clearly, if the ministry responds to all of these requests, it is responding to member church needs as well as to the needs of the community. Such programming for the churches generally takes up only a fraction of the time and resources of a community ministry, but it remains an important part of the total program because it builds and strengthens the foundations of the organization upon which the community-directed programs depend. With that qualification, response to the needs of a specific community is the major function of community ministry.

Operating on a small scale, community ministry may assess needs through a variety of informal and formal means. Ideas for programs and projects may stem from pastoral staffs (professional and volunteer), active members of the churches, other organizations with which the ministry has working relations, and formal processes for needs assessment and community analysis.

Pastoral Staff

Pastoral staff may provide the best community needs analysis to be found. Contrary to notions that pastoral concerns are irrelevant to community ministry or that pastoral counseling deals only with individuals, many programs trace their roots to pastors who saw implications for community ministry in the problems of individuals. DOVE, the program mentioned in chapter I, put a priority on the problem of domestic violence. That priority was confirmed when pastors began seeking advice regarding counselees who were victims or abusers. Several ministries have come into the field of services for the elderly because pastors called for an ecumenical approach to those needs.

At St. MAM, a program for families affected by chemical dependency and codependency was initiated after pastors said that as much as 90 percent of pastoral care problems were related to the abuse of alcohol. Across the country, community organization projects have sprung from essentially pastoral concerns—over the provision of government-funded services, adequate housing, decisions about development and zoning, or the inability of emergency-assistance clients to pay utility bills.

Church Members

Many church members are involved in projects for improving the quality of life and in causes on behalf of the poor. Some seek to promote justice within the business or institution where they work. Some are themselves victims of discriminatory and unjust systems. Others may be trying their best to respond to denominational exhortations to work for peace or for sane ecological practices. Taken together, these persons represent energy and resources already being spent in the exercise of community ministry.

A member of the board of St. MAM who had been instrumental in starting self-help groups became aware of the problem of child sexual abuse. In an annual planning session, she made a case for the community ministry to take up the cause. Staff of the organization had encountered the problem in a number of contexts, and they supported her plea. The ministry started a task force on child sexual abuse that quickly became a resource for the entire region as well as for the immediate area. It resulted in the formation of the first Parents United chapter in the state of Kentucky.

It should not be taken for granted that activist church members will take an interest in community ministry. Some will have to be persuaded that a very local form of social ministry is needed. As a practical matter, many will not have the surplus time and energy to give to a new ministry, and it is to the credit of community ministry that it tends to recruit entirely fresh personnel to ministry, many of whom would otherwise not become involved in it. But one should not underestimate the contribution that socially concerned church members can and will make to program development if persuaded to do so.

Networks

Local networks of cooperation become matrices for detection of need and program development. In the late 1960s and early 1970s, community ministries commonly helped runaway and wandering youth who were alienated from their families and traditional youth-serving structures. The Ministries, a community ministry on Long Island, undertook to develop, along with other youth-serving agencies, a directory of services for youth. Young people who were both clients and volunteers at the ministry supplied a list of questions as well as the language that would speak to the current youth culture. The directory was so popular among youth and so successful in directing youth to various facilities and resources that it went through several editions. Then the cooperating agencies suggested that the ministry take the lead in putting out a second directory, which would be for the use of agencies and their staff. This directory, which was also well received and widely read, precipitated the development of a referral network among youth-serving agencies, which is still operating years later. All of this resulted in cooperative engagement in several programs, with one agency taking the lead in each case. Because the ministry had Spanish-speaking staff, it was asked to assist in starting a program for the youth of a predominantly Hispanic neighborhood. Then . . . well, the story could go on almost indefinitely. This all emanated from one rather modest cooperative project!

In the almost overwhelming atmosphere of unrest among youth in the late 60s and early 70s, the various youth-serving agencies of Suffolk County, Long Island, found that through cooperation they could more effectively meet the needs they were intended to fulfill. Cooperation increases effectiveness in nearly every instance, but it is sometimes only obvious in situations where the need is greatest.

There are some indications that we are again entering a period of social dislocation of large numbers of youth, and today the same dynamic is affecting Emergency Financial Assistance (EFA) programs. Community ministries and EFA agencies are discovering the need to communicate regularly and cooperate to establish new programs, set up networks for regular consultation, advocate an end to governmental retreat in the field, and combat an overemphasis on EFA at the expense of other programs.

Formal Needs Assessment and Community Analyses

A statistical-demographic approach will produce a more or less objective profile of the mission area relative to other areas or to general population statistics. Such a document is sometimes necessary for writing grant proposals and may be used to substantiate statements of need or to interpret the ministry's work. It might include inferences already drawn from the data by government planning agencies, businesses and churches, or other organizations. Government agencies will sometimes provide charts and maps showing the implications of the data for various sectors, systems, and areas. Developers of retailing complexes often prepare rather detailed descriptions of marketing areas that contain interesting if not essential information. Law enforcement agencies and utility companies have potentially valuable data. At least one denomination (the United Church of Christ) will send its congregations a compendium of census data for the census tracts requested by the congregation. The information is organized for purposes of congregational planning and can be useful for community ministry as well. Some Catholic dioceses have planners who collect descriptive data parish by parish.

The most recent and revolutionary development in this field is the production for business marketing purposes of block-by-block profiles based on credit purchases. There are people translating this data for the benefit of church planners. Many helpful contacts will be made in collecting data from the above sources, and the people who locate the data may have some interesting observations.

The demographic profile will help a community ministry define the boundaries of its area of mission "at the most local level possible"—that is, to define a community or potential community with which the ministry can identify on a daily and personal basis and which is also large enough to sustain its own community ministry.

Academic Studies

Institutions of higher education can be of assistance in analyzing an area. Administrators, students, and faculty will be interested if the project relates to their particular role in a college or graduate school. Ministries sometimes engage faculty on a volunteer or consulting basis. DOVE engaged a sociologist from Millikin University through a grant from the Community Council on Private Higher Education, which places faculty interns in community-based projects. A study of the area by a social-work class may help give a sense of place to those who live and work there.

In fact, such class projects at the Carver School of Social Work at Southern Baptist Theological Seminary in Louisville have been known to instigate conversations about starting a community ministry. Ministries United of South Central Louisville owes its beginnings to such a study. Classes in sociology, social relations, psychology, medicine, and public health as well as religion or theology are all potential sources of analyses.

Do not expect too much from academic studies. Some needs are simply inaccessible to even the best classroom methods. The relationships established by these studies might be as important as the studies themselves.

Feasibility Studies

Fund-raising feasibility studies are a form of needs assessment. A feasibility study is ordinarily conducted before a major fund-raising effort, and when administered by a reliable consultant, it will contain valuable data. The consultant has an interest in finding out just what claims the people of a community are willing to make upon a ministry and on what basis the ministry has a chance of achieving permanence in the community. Even when a ministry decides not to go ahead with a fund drive, it can still use the feasibility study for program-development purposes.

Cooperative Needs Assessment

A community ministry might organize a cooperative needs assessment project. For example, a women's club put up funds to employ for a summer a social worker who was to assess the needs of youth by hanging out with them, interviewing them, keeping a journal, and writing a summary report. The "Y" had a place that the worker could use as a base, the community ministry was responsible for supervision, and a federally funded regional social services provider wrote up the results in a report. The report made a strong case for a community youth services program that was eventually established by the community ministry.

Further Observations About Needs Assessment

Following are some further observations about assessing social needs in the context of community ministry.

First, the value of this context for the disciplines that might embrace it (missiology, ecumenics, sociology, practical theology, ekistics (the science of human settlements), human services, community development, social relations) is that it helps to discover what is actually going on at the grassroots. There is a wealth of information available through community ministry about the character of daily life at the most local level. This is why community ministries at times have been besieged by graduate students and questionnaires far beyond their capacity to respond. This is also why some state and metropolitan ecumenical groupings (in Washington, Texas, and Kentucky, for example) are intentional about listening to community ministries as they make decisions about programs and projects.

Second, although pastors are good sources of information about needs, there have been few means to help them cultivate their potential or reflect upon it. Community ministry is such a means. Pastors have an important role as observers of the community. Through community ministry, they may be among the most important agents of needs assessment.

Third, the establishment of an information and referral (I&R) service produces a "built-in" needs-assessment system. By recording all I&R calls, updating files on services available, and following up on all referrals, I&R can identify gaps in various systems. In these times, when many community ministries have been set up specifically to deliver emergency assistance, the very least such a community ministry can do is to start an I&R program. I&R is an essential companion to emergency assistance because it causes the ministry to deal with the inquirer in a holistic way; to make some positive response to every question; to become aware of needed programs, projects, and advocacies other than emergency assistance; and to work cooperatively with other ministries and agencies. In short, I&R points emergency assistance in the direction of a more complete social ministry.

Fourth, one of the more interesting and unexplored aspects of community ministry is its capacity to be a sensor of social needs before they are generally known or recognized. In 1984, before national attention had been focused on the problem of child sexual abuse, this form of abuse was encountered in three programs of a single community ministry within a period of several months. Parents came to enroll their children in the ministry's childcare program after the private program their children had previously been enrolled in became the subject of allegations and litigation. (The ministry arranged training for its staff for relating to those children.) The problem also arose in the counseling service of the youth services program. Another connection was found in the ministry's drug-and-alcohol-intervention service. A community-wide task force was formed that was a first for that area. This "sensing" function may be related to the fact that community ministry does not take its cue from national or regional priority setting processes. Its priorities emerge in the day-to-day interplay of people and events in their neighborhoods.

Style and Response

There are many ways by which organizations proceed from defining a need to taking action. How they decide to make the connection partly determines their unique identity and character, their particular style of social ministry.

Setting Priorities

The basis for the relative independence of community ministry is the support of its congregations. The responsible use of this liberty depends upon a ministry's fashioning its own criteria for action. A clear purpose with a process for setting priorities makes the ministry something more than a reflection of the community it serves.

The process may include asking certain questions: What do those who will benefit from the ministry say? Is this ministry the logical agency to respond, or could another do it better? Will this new project complement other activities of the ministry?

Will there be financial support for it? Is it an opportunity to work cooperatively?

By engaging in a discussion of this sort, a ministry will increase "ownership" among board members who are ultimately responsible for the ministry's actions. It will establish a balance among immediate claims, those of the past reflected in current programming, and those of the future now unforeseen. It will guard against "opportunity management"—that is, starting a program merely because work is there to be done.

Types of Response

Responses can range from a one-time educational event to direct social action to a program entailing several years of effort. In general, we can divide responses into two categories: projects of limited duration and programs of open-ended duration. Thus a project may result in a program, or a program may include several projects. Community ministry benefits from flexibility with regard to these categories since the important thing is to fit the response to the particular community and need.

The tendency will be to justify the organization's existence by the development and maintenance of ongoing programs. This mentality results in the uncritical continuation of programs until they die a slow death or the funding for them disappears. There are ways to combat this "justification by program" syndrome. Programs can be evaluated at regular intervals as to whether they should continue or take another form. Programs can be "given" to the community when they are taken over by another agency or become independent. It may be easier to tout programs than projects, but the virtues of flexibility and "traveling light" certainly will be recognized in the churches and in the community.

Some leaders feel ministries should preserve flexibility by avoiding long-term maintenance of programs that could function just as well on their own or under other auspices. Others, like Stan Esterle of Highlands Community Ministries, believe that "if community ministry wants to work with persons in a holistic way, then the more programs it can maintain the better.

Programs will contribute to each other in many ways; and the 'bottom line' is that cooperation among programs of the same ministry will benefit the people being served while also insuring that all the programs work cooperatively rather than compete with one another."[8] Esterle thinks that, in his particular setting (a conglomeration of urban neighborhoods), ongoing programs are generally the best response.

The point is that each community ministry chooses its own style. It is important that it do so intentionally. Depending on the situation, social ministry may be as much a matter of how things are done as it is of what things are done.

The Value of Cooperation

In principle, community ministry responds to need in ways that raise the level of cooperation among all the organizations that have some interest or role vis-à-vis the need that is being addressed. Not all agencies will reciprocate, but the rule is to assume that all the relevant and interested organizations want to cooperate.

Few Resources Are Not a Barrier

Community ministries are less dependent than many organizations on the availability of staff, plant, and money when they decide whether or how to respond to a need. It is not that such things are not taken into consideration, but community ministry generally has access to competent and experienced volunteers who can carry a program forward until paid staff come onto the scene. Moreover, community ministry often can "borrow" staff from churches or other agencies for the initial stages of a program. It can also find people who will take positions for limited periods without guarantee of regular employment. Normally, rent is the largest nonsalary expense in a first-year budget. However, the availability of church facilities may ease the burden in this respect as well.

Lack of funds, space and staff will play a lesser role because community ministry is an extension of the ministries of many congregations. Once the need has been established and the decision to respond has been made, there is good reason to be optimistic about finding the wherewithal to begin.

Varieties of Response

What is most striking about successful programs is that they not only respond to some particular need, they also increase the organization's capacity for response. These "programs" are really channels of program development.

A *volunteer service corps*. South East Associated Ministries in Louisville hired an experienced director of volunteers and proceeded to develop a uniquely effective series of programs based on capability for volunteer service. These were volunteer-intensive programs such as the Life-Skills Center through which volunteers assisted local residents with practical problems, including budgeting, homemaking, and parenting. The same ministry started a bloodmobile program in cooperation with the Red Cross and utilized dozens of volunteers from the churches. This is both a participatory and ministry-of-the-laity approach toward program development. The more people that can be recruited into a particular response, the better. Eventually the Life-Skills Center received a grant for its continuance, but this approach is notable for its lack of dependence on such funds. Moreover, if successful, it results in a critical mass of members of churches working together, that is, in large enough numbers to make the ministry a cohesive factor among the churches and in the community. In this case a rather nebulous area of subdivisions, apartment buildings, and strip shopping centers began to recognize itself as a community.

Community organization. Quite a different tack was taken by Highlands Community Ministries in the early 1970s. It formed organizations for each of the neighborhoods within its community (in some cases their first task was to name their neighborhood). These organizations are independent from the ministry, although the executive director chairs a regular meeting of their representatives. Thanks to these organizations, the ministries have never

wanted for agenda items or proposed courses of action. Sometimes the churches have found themselves at odds with one or
more of the community organizations (for example, over rezoning
requests to expand church parking lots). On the other hand, when
the ministry wanted to build housing for elderly and Disabled
people on the site of a neighborhood softball diamond, the
neighbors on the street opposed the plan, but the neighborhood
association's support was instrumental in the success of the project. In any case, the community organizations have been an in-
valuable forum for the airing of concerns in the community.

Links to pastoral care. Some ministries build systematically and
intentionally on the link between pastoral care and social ministry. At St. MAM, a parishioner came to her pastor to ask his assistance in advocating a new approach in dealing with drug and
alcohol abuse. She was referred to another pastor because of
his connection to the ministry. Then, in an informal discussion
among members of the pastoral staffs of the member churches
of the community ministry, some pastors expressed their conviction that alcoholism and other forms of chemical dependency were implicated in a large percentage of the problems
they encountered in pastoral counseling. The ministry's executive director and the parishioner drew up a proposal that was
then considered by a committee made up of people picked for
their expertise and interest in the field. Eventually the board of
directors approved a new program for that community based on
a new approach to overcoming chemical dependency. For four
consecutive years, both the budget and number of persons
served (who were served regardless of ability to pay) doubled.
At the end of the period, the program became the outpatient
component of a chemical dependency program of a hospital in
the community. In the meantime, hundreds of families received
more meaningful and effective help for these problems than
they had ever experienced before—all because the churches of
the community were seeking a cooperative solution to a pressing pastoral concern.

Pilot programming. The Ministries of Suffolk County, Long Island, located on the perimeter of metropolitan New York, was

started as a kind of showcase experiment by several denominations in the late 1960s. As a result—although the stimulus for its programs has been the local community—it has sought to choose programs that are national in scope and importance. Thus the first program undertaken by The Ministries was Suffolk Housing Services, a housing opportunity center that was to address the problems of housing discrimination in that community and to have an impact on the national scene. The Kerner Report had just been published, raising the specter of a United States with two unequal and divided societies within its borders. The center received funding from national foundations to conduct an ambitious program of litigation (including test cases) on behalf of fair and low-income housing. A large local clientele was a critical factor in the center's becoming a focal point for such litigation. It permitted the ministry to develop expertise in the problems that people face in finding housing, build credibility in the eyes of national funding sources, accumulate a data base for its litigation activities, and gain support in the community and its churches for its national activities. Developing a program with a national impact is always an option for community ministry. It requires, however, the involvement of people whose scope of activity includes both the local and the national. Moreover, its local orientation and impact must be capable of withstanding the intense scrutiny that comes with national attention. Such was and is the fortunate situation of Suffolk Housing Services.

Justice and Localism

How do community ministries respond to those claims for justice that by definition transcend localities? Can they contribute to a global agenda of peace or to a national agenda for improving social structures? Although community ministry has the potential for carrying the claims of justice into the heart of local communities, it is not yet clear whether the potential will be realized. There are three challenges before community ministry at this moment: to link the local and the global, to learn how to speak prophetically, and to expand the capacity for social action.

Linking the Global and Local

No matter how locally rooted a congregation is, the international dimension is one of its givens. The churches receive numerous reminders connecting local and global concerns. In fact, the global reach of denominations or faith groups represented in the community is justification enough for the airing of global concerns. If, during the course of discussions, implications are drawn for action in the local community, so much the better.

Certain programs carry an inherent connection between global and local. In Louisville, St. MAM has operated a temporary hostel for international students during the Christmas and New Year's holidays. It has also resettled refugees in cooperation with Church World Service and Catholic Charities.

It is becoming increasingly difficult to separate global from local concerns. The rapid diffusion of information to large populations, the interdependence of economies, and the sharing of a common and deteriorating environment have all brought us to this point where, for example, in the villages of Latin America the dependence on North America is acutely felt and named as such. Liberation theology, which stresses the fundamental religious significance of the local community, makes this reality one of its points of departure. The crucial role of local religious coalitions in the breakup of communist hegemony in eastern Europe (Berlin, Leipzig, Timisoara) is evidence to support this view. It is becoming more obvious that in certain situations justice requires making the global connections explicit.

Further, there are increasing opportunities to gain an understanding of the wider context through the local experience. In the field of theological education, for example, we witness an interest in "contextual learning." San Francisco Network Ministries in the Tenderloin district of San Francisco has become a focal point for theological education in that area. In general, whenever a community ministry is located near an institution of theological education, it becomes an important field education site. In San Francisco this relationship has developed to the point that students and faculty do on-site reflection and study together. The community ministry's area of mission, rather than the more traditional classroom elements, is providing the underlying educational rationale. Thus, this community ministry has itself become an educational institution, a demonstration of the significance of the local community for understanding the wider contexts.

Being Locally Rooted and Prophetic

Whenever a community ministry says a critical or prophetic word about its community, it risks its continued existence; this is true for any stance that might cause offense in the community. Yet it would not be a social ministry if it ignored the claims of justice for the sake of its own survival, and there would be little to distinguish it from myriad social service organizations. We are presented with a basic dilemma of community ministry when the interests of survival as a local institution conflict with claims of justice.

It is not in the interest of the churches or of the community to have a fence-sitting ministry in its midst. For the churches, the raison d'être of their participation is their desire to exercise a social ministry locally, meaning that they want to do those things, among others, that cannot be expressed by the term *social service*. What would those things be if they did not include speaking and doing the prophetic word? The larger community's acceptance of a community ministry is predicated on the notion that a community ministry has a certain capacity or freedom to accomplish things for the whole community that governmental or other private agencies do not possess. What better way to exemplify this special capacity than through a prophetic word?

Those who would attempt to maintain a community ministry that avoids the claims of justice ought to be forewarned of the difficulty of such a project. Individuals and groups within the churches will bring the burdens of justice to the doorstep of the ministry. Such claims—coming as they will from the backbone of the ministry, the congregations themselves—cannot be denied thorough consideration. Events will occur in the community that call for some response and/or interpretation by the community ministry. When an act of vandalism is committed with racist implications, what does a community ministry do or say? It is on the spot in a way that metropolitan-wide and national human rights organizations are not. Community organizations representing all or part of the community will put their issues on the agenda of the ministry. Community organizations may be one solution to the dilemma of community ministry because they have the potential for opening timid community ministries to the claims of justice. Fortunate is the community ministry that has a parallel community organization within its mission area with which—or against which—it may battle. There will be occasions when community organizations act on behalf of the entire community vis-à-vis larger structures, and it would be important for the community ministry to be a part of that advocacy. There will also be occasions when an issue divides the community or puts the activity of the community ministry into question. In such cases one must remember that divisions in the community or in the ministry are not caused by the community organization! The community organization only brings the divisions out into the open where they can be dealt with justly.

Social Action

Social action has been a key element of community ministry since the first congregation invited Jew and Greek, slave and free, male and female to worship together. By "social action" we mean actions by a religious or other group to change the structures of society. Thus social action is not necessarily implied either in linking the global and local or in speaking prophetically, since it is quite possible to deal with specific global-local linkages or specific issues of community organization without ever challenging the structures of society. Social action, therefore, may be the most controversial part of community ministry, implying as it does, a radical critique of existing economic, political, and social arrangements. Yet social action always will be a part of community ministry as long as societies do not approach perfection. In the bosom of every religious community there exists that radical critique that is the basis for social action. In 1989 we witnessed a dramatic example of the role that religious groups played in changing the political landscape of eastern Europe.

How does community ministry participate in social action? A challenge to engagement might come from any of the sources we cited in the previous paragraphs, but most often the impetus toward social action stems from the frustrations of community ministry in trying to help individuals get out of desperate circumstances. For example, in the winter of 1982, several community ministries in the Louisville area were besieged by people seeking emergency assistance. Within one year the funds funneled though community ministry for this purpose quadrupled. Upon analysis, it was found that 80 percent of the funds were spent to stop utility cutoffs that can lead to illness and death and to prevent the loss of housing itself—often the result of rising utility costs. When governmental stop-gap measures failed to stem the tide of suffering and distress, several community ministries in Louisville supported a drive to change the system by which households paid for their utilities. A "percentage of income" plan was advocated so that no household with an income below a certain level would be required to pay more than a certain percentage of its income for energy costs.

The ministries found funds to pay for organizers and lobbyists to present the plan to the next session of the state legislature—but to no avail. The utility companies mobilized hundreds of lobbyists against the effort. Some of the ministries experienced pressure from utility company management through the boards and councils of their member congregations. But it is characteristic of such efforts not to crumble after the first (or fourth, in this case) try. At this writing, the effort continues and seems to be making progress in spite of overwhelming odds. This experience has proven to community ministries of one area that they can engage in effective social action.

These struggles derive primarily from problems encountered in the delivery of services to individuals and the frustrations involved in making the system work. The claims of justice are not likely to be satisfied by your best efforts on behalf of a single issue or person in need. However, those efforts in any vital community ministry may propel you into the social action arena.

Exceptions to the Rule

Social action requires two significant qualifications of the principle of "ministry at the most local level possible." First, in order to change systems, one generally has to work at a level of larger scope than the neighborhood. In fact, in many cases a ministry will feel compelled to move to the statewide level. In the field of housing, for example, it is imperative to implement strategies on all levels, including the national.

The second qualification is related to the first: In order to change systems, a community ministry should ally itself with other ministries and organizations that are experiencing the same frustrations and have the same conviction of the need to change systems. In any case, a wider coalition with a social change agenda will be the stronger for having the neighborhood base that community ministry brings to it.

An Admonition

An important question of justice exists in relationships among community ministries. In some communities it is financially impossible to achieve a staffed community ministry based on the support of area congregations and parishes. Furthermore, once established, some ministries command many more resources than others. In the name of justice, community ministry must face these inequalities squarely and find ways to minimize them. The point of departure for this discussion would be the following problem: How can available resources be shared in such a way that community ministry becomes possible in every locality where the churches desire to start such a ministry? This approach implies at least an informal organization on a regional or metropolitan basis and cooperation between community ministries for developing resources.

3   Redefining the Ecumenical Movement

AROUND 1967, local congregations and parishes began to discover that—imperceptibly—many of the barriers to cooperation in their neighborhood or rural area had fallen. At first, we attributed these developments to Vatican II, which brought an infusion of Catholic energies into the ecumenical movement.[9] From the vantage point of today we can see that although Vatican II was an important factor, other developments such as ecumenical/interfaith marriages and the free movement of individuals among congregations without respect to historic differences may have been even more important. In any case, the result is that many differences of belief, practice, culture, and style that once characterized denominations are no longer owned by their members. Now it seems that differences between congregations stem more from their unique history than from denominational identity.

Community Ministry—A Case in Point

The community ministry movement may be the chief illustration of this new context for intercongregational relations; as such, it represents a challenge to the older ecumenical movement. In fact, one could imagine a confrontation that would be harmful both to the cause of social justice and to the quest for Christian unity. The situation, therefore, calls for a reorientation of the ecumenical movement to embrace the new local ecumenism.

Congregations Take the Lead

The community ministries movement reflects a revival of respect for the congregation as a religious institution. We even may be witnessing the formation of a new mainstream ecumenism based on clusters of congregations. The new situation holds an opportunity for the ecumenical movement.

In community ministry we have experienced firsthand, and for some time, that which the relatively new field of congregational studies[10] is now articulating for us. Our work requires a view of the congregation that rules out the judgmental mind-set that dominated higher education and the condescension that permeated American intellectual life for so long. These attitudes viewed congregational life across the country as monolithic, trivial, and uninteresting. In every community ministry we accept a variety of congregations, each with its own story, language, culture, style, and role, and we positively respect each congregation for its uniqueness.

Wherever one finds a community ministry, there are congregations that have intentionally come together in spite of their differences (about which we now have a greater appreciation, thanks to the congregational studies field) to cooperate for the sake of the community. Upon reflection, this is a remarkable commitment that could serve as the foundation for renewal of the ecumenical movement.

Growing Independence of Congregations

The formation of community ministries throughout the country is taking place against the backdrop of initiative taking on the part of congregations. This self-assertion may be taken as an extension of voluntaristic religion as described by Wade Clark Roof and William McKinney: "Typically Americans view religious congregations as gatherings of individuals who have chosen to be together in institutions of their own making and over which they hold control—fostering what sometimes, in the eyes of observers of other countries, appears as 'churchless Christianity'."[11]

If this is an accurate description, then people are joining congregations because it seems best for them but without the implication that it would be best for everyone. It says that certain congregations suit certain people better than others, that each congregation has its own function or place in the community, and that congregations' claims to be unique possessors of the truth are not to be taken seriously except insofar as they reflect the needs of the people who choose those congregations. It explains why it has become relatively easy for disparate congregations to form community ministries. They may join without fear that either their uniqueness or the claims of their denomination will be challenged. The uniqueness of each will be seen as desirable and the claims of the denomination will be viewed as largely irrelevant.

The Expanding Spectrum of Local Cooperation

It may be the case that the more local the scope, the broader the spectrum of cooperation. True, the larger the area, the greater the variety of religious affiliations; yet the smaller the area, the greater the incentive for the various groups that are there to cooperate because of the immediacy of local problems and identification with a common locality. For example, in many cities, the traditional ecumenical organization celebrates the fact of Catholic or Southern Baptist participation—a real plus since these two are such large faith communities. But these groups have already been participating for twenty years in neighborhood-based community ministries along with Church of God, Church of Christ, Church of Jesus Christ of Latter-day Saints, Eastern Orthodox, Lutheran Church Missouri Synod, Cumberland Presbyterian, and Christian Science congregations—and others not hitherto noted for ecumenical participation.

Interfaith Ministries

Among the first community ministries organized in the 1960s were some that found themselves in the vanguard of interfaith relations because they included synagogues in their membership

(The Ministries of Suffolk County, Long Island, for example). But some community ministries have defined themselves in such explicitly Christian terms that it would be difficult for a congregation of another faith to participate. Some have set up special programs or divisions for interfaith discussions and activity. On the other hand, some have constituted themselves as interfaith organizations (United Ministries of Greenville, South Carolina; South Hills Interfaith Ministries of Bethel Park, Pennsylvania; and East Side Interfaith Ministries of Cleveland, for example). The nationally organized Interfaith Network of Community Ministries decided to include the term *interfaith* in its name in recognition that, increasingly, community ministries are seeking interfaith participation.

Unquestionably, community ministries are experiencing tension in the choices between the words *cooperative, ecumenical,* and *interfaith*. The resolution of these issues may lie more in how one defines the local community than in an ideology of community ministry. Community ministries will become more inclusive in both ecumenical and interfaith relations to the extent that specific communities have that character. Based on the record heretofore, it would be surprising to find a community ministry described as a force for religious exclusivism, but an informed answer to this question awaits the passage of more time and the accumulation of more experience.

Ecumenism Is No Longer a Clergy Preserve

Community ministry might be seen as a breakthrough for the laity, because before the onset of our movement even the more ecumenically minded clergy tended to take a proprietary attitude toward anything having to do with relationships between churches. In fact, the presence of a ministerial association still might not bode well for the establishment of a community ministry since the association might view itself as the ecumenical presence in the community. It is often the assumption even in traditional ecumenism that it is the clergy's function to represent religious groups to the outside. Hence, the ecumenical movement had been largely in the hands of religious professionals.

Most community ministries, however, are led by a predominantly lay board and a staff that may or may not include ministers and other theologically trained persons. Some community ministries prefer executive leadership that is ordained, but at least as many opt for persons trained in fields other than theology. In general, ministries prefer staff that are actively involved in a faith community but not necessarily trained as religious professionals.

The principle that clergy determine ecumenical relationships is modified but not overturned in community ministry. For example, at Central Hillside United Ministry in Duluth, Minnesota, pastors are automatically members of the board by virtue of their office, whereas the laity are either elected by their congregations or appointed by their pastor. Even this kind of modification will be too much for some clergy who want to defend their traditional prerogatives in the field of ecumenical relations. Clearly, the community ministry movement is redefining the role of clergy in the community. It may be rare for a community ministry to get started without the planning and nurturing of professional ministers, but these are the special ministers who place a high value on the participation of the laity within the total framework of the churches' ministry. In case after case, we observe such ministers stepping aside as the people of their congregations fill leadership roles. Then the task of the ministry is to negotiate the reentry of clergy into the work. Both North Dallas Shared Ministries and Corpus Christi Metro Ministries find themselves—at this writing—with almost no clergy participation, whereas clergy were instrumental in their inception. Now they seek to find ways to elicit interest on the part of clergy. This challenge is typical. William Thomas of the Mon Valley Ministries of Duquesne, Pennsylvania, puts a priority on clergy participation. He says, "Clergy, like everyone else, bring their own unique gifts to community ministries. Especially in smaller churches clergy have a variety of skills that are not fully utilized. But put them into the larger context of community ministry and they will be more likely to apply all the skills at their command."[12]

The ministry of the laity movement has contributed to the growth of community ministry. It is noteworthy that although most community ministries appear to have been started by the initiative of clergy, closer scrutiny almost always reveals an initiative by the laity. Church members, in taking stock of their gifts for ministry, now sometimes come to the conclusion that they are, in fact, "community ministers." Typically, a community ministry receives several calls each year from those who—upon reflection—have decided to try community ministry as a medium for their own ministry.

At St. MAM, new board members are reminded that every Christian has a part in the mission of the church by virtue of his or her baptism and that their part may be done ecumenically because of their congregation's participation in community ministry. Through interpretations of this sort, community ministry is affecting the ministry of the laity movement. It illustrates the fact that ministry is not an either/or proposition (either in the church as teacher, leader, etc., or outside at the place of daily work). On the contrary, ministry may be both/and—both in the congregation and outside through a community ministry that is an extension of the congregation.

Thus, for individuals engaged in it, community ministry is a special kind of personal ministry. A government worker, for example, might discover that a community ministry is a potential ally in her effort to improve some human service delivery system. On the other hand, a member of the parish council may find that his involvement in community ministry enhances his contribution to the work of the council. This kind of ministry straddles the boundary between church and society and cannot be pigeonholed into one or the other.

Therefore, encouraging a broadened view of the ministry of the laity is a significant ecumenical role for community ministry among its member congregations. This support may extend to organizing lay ministry training. Some denominations are producing extraordinarily fine materials in this field, and community ministry can help bring these materials alive.

Interdisciplinary Relations—Social Work

In community ministry there is an ecumenicity of disciplines. It engages all who occupy themselves with the concept of local community. The churches have a reciprocal relationship with the social work profession, for example. They benefit from the skills of this profession and from its long relationship to the field of social ministry. And, conversely, community ministry contributes something to the social work profession insofar as it is not possible for a social worker to function adequately in community ministry without a commitment to that particular community and to the principle of the churches doing social ministry collectively in one place. Generalizations about the delivery of social services, which may have currency within the discipline, must be reexamined in the light of the community being served. Thus the social work profession, as it engages the churches through community ministry, admits the concepts of "parish" and "pastoral action" into its universe of thought.

Relations with Other Fields

The same reciprocity has been experienced in other fields of research and training, among them education, health, and sociology. The point is that community ministry does not depend exclusively upon the generalizations of one discipline or profession. We respond above all to the reality of the community itself. In the name of the community, we take an eclectic approach.

This ecumenicity of disciplines may be possible only at the most local level. There, the disciplines' favorite fads are vulnerable to the community itself and to the other disciplines as well. To be sure, the style of an earlier ecumenism was to use the various disciplines, in reaching goals, but it stopped short of bringing them together in determining goals in the first place. In community ministry a potpourri of educational backgrounds is essential for a complete response to the community. Thus, a community ministry staff might include degree holders and non–degree holders (with skills obtained through experience) in teaching, social work, psychology, religion, and many other fields. Its board might be expected to embrace a similar variety of credentials, including those of having needed or used its programs.

Growth in Ecumenical/Interfaith Funding

The financing of community ministry is another indication of the changing ecumenical scene. The new ecumenism has brought tens of millions of new dollars annually into the broadly defined ecumenical field.

Although a typical community ministry may not be able to project secure funding of its operations more than six months into the future, these ministries are channels for an incredible flow of financial support from the society at large into church-related work. In Louisville, for example, the budget of the Council of Churches in 1966 was approximately $40,000. That amount, plus some settlement house programs sponsored by individual churches, pretty much represented the total amount available for all the ecumenical work and all the church-based social ministry of the metropolitan area. Today, the budget of the successor organization of the Council of Churches is only slightly more than it was then. The combined budgets of the community ministries in the area, however, total about $5.2 million—$250,000 of which are local church funds.[13] If one ignored the community ministries, one might conclude that there had been a decline in ecumenical finances. But these figures show that, far from being in decline, ecumenical dollars have been growing at the most local level since the mid-1960s.

Local Participation Produces Joint Funding

The secret of this funding "success" (one would be hard put to convince individual community ministries that they were part of a funding success!) is the reality of local cooperation. Community ministry places a claim on the increasing percentage of philanthropic, governmental, and church dollars that are destined to be spent locally. Because of their local orientation, the finances of community ministries are no secret! This fact results in opportunities for interpretation that lead to still more participation.

More problematic from the standpoint of ecumenical relations is the fact that probably 40 percent of the new funds ultimately come from government sources.[14] In some areas (for example, in Texas) community ministry struggles to maintain an ecumenical identity not obscured by the fact that it is part of the delivery system of the state department of human services.

Implications of the New Ecumenism

Local Experience and Acceptance of Ecumenical/Social Ministry

The negativism one finds in congregations toward national and international ecumenical structures stems partly from the fact that many congregations have not yet experienced ecumenical social ministry at the congregational level. Such lack of experience magnifies the problem of interpreting nationwide and worldwide ecumenical social ministry. However, as congregations cooperate in social ministry within a community, they are more likely to accept social ministry as an essential aspect of the total ministry of the church.

Whatever differences continue to separate denominations, they carry no more weight as justification for separate social ministries on the local level than they do at the national and international levels. One of the most blatant contradictions in denominationalism is the manner in which denominations undercut their national and international commitments by doing ecumenical social ministry only at those levels. (The most recent restructuring of the National Council of Churches actually reduces the staff and funding for local ecumenism.)[15] If denominations would encourage more ecumenical social ministry at the most local level possible, their commitment at the other levels would gain more credibility.

One Ecumenical Movement or Two?

The community ministries movement remains at some distance from the ecumenical movement. It is edifying, however, to speculate on what the result would be were the two movements to converge. Community ministry might well go down as a new chapter in the history of the social gospel, developing into a training ground for effective social action by congregations, promoting intercultural understanding, improving relations between congregations and communities, and developing educational programs of interfaith and interdenominational interest. Because of its highly local character, community ministry might attract a greater proportion of available church resources for a social ministry that is effective, compassionate, and self-critical—one that is planned, implemented, and supported on a local and ecumenical basis.

Nonclergy leaders would find their contribution as valued as that of clergy in the context of community ministry. Individuals who held peripheral status because of their enthusiasm for social ministry would be fully accepted into community ministry along with the leadership core of congregations. Localities would come into focus as fields of mission for which congregations accept responsibility. Social ministry would attain a new status as part of a total and indigenous ministry. Good relationships among churches would be cultivated for the sake of a joint social mission. Churches in a given area would aspire to cooperation, service, and advocacy on behalf of building a community where justice and peace are hallmarks.

If this happy convergence does not happen, community ministry could turn in a quite different and reactionary direction. It might, in the name of localism, oppose ecumenical mission in its national and international expressions and begrudge the sharing of resources with the global community. It might, in the name of direct service to needy individuals, oppose the social advocacies that would seek systemic change. It might, in the name of "cooperation," oppose the goal of Christian unity and accept as a given the denominational system with its enshrined distinctions of class and race as well as those of doctrine and practice. They might, in the name of preserving their social prestige, espouse an uncritical patriotism, relegating the prophetic voices to the far edges of the churches.

In this latter scenario, the community ministry movement would appear as little more than the social service arm of a right-of-center political and economic ideology. It would be anti-ecumenical both in the sense of discouraging any attempt to heal the fragmentation of religious institutions and in the sense of refusing to entertain practical and theoretical linkages between local and international issues. It would be antisocial except insofar as the term might be used to describe direct service and ameliorative action.

These contrasting possible futures reveal how a movement so full of potential in ecumenical relations and social ministry could become a reactionary societal force. It shows how unpredictable the movement is. This uncertainty must be addressed eventually by all those concerned with ecumenical and social ministry.

Mutual Influence of the Ecumenical Movement and Community Ministry

Fortunately, the ecumenical and community ministry movements have influenced each other in recent years. By 1960, many councils of churches had become preoccupied with maintaining established programs that represented the self-interest of the religious community taken as a whole—priorities that were generated in meetings of regional denominational leaders. As these councils and their successors have interacted with community ministry, they have become more sensitive to priorities at the most local level. The Kentucky, Ohio, Minnesota, Indiana, and Texas councils of churches have encouraged new community ministries. Two arms of the ecumenical movement, the Ecumenical Networks Working Group (formerly the Commission on Regional and Local Ecumenism) of the National Council of Churches and the National Association of Ecumenical Staff, have made efforts to include community ministry in their structures.

On their side, community ministries certainly have felt the influence of the ecumenical movement. In 1970, community ministry typically limited itself to social ministry. In that year Long Island's The Ministries engaged in fair-housing efforts, consumer advocacy, alternative information and referral systems, youth advocacy, draft counseling, criminal justice reform, child care, community-based arts and education, a food pantry, and still other social ministry programs. It had little interest in church-related networks outside of its immediate area of service, and it was frankly antipathetic toward the established ecumenical movement. The community ministry of the 1980s, however, was more apt to initiate programs seeking to improve relations among the member churches and denominations—such as clergy lunches and use of "faith and order" materials. Highlands Community Ministries in Louisville instituted a formal covenantal relationship among its churches. Some community ministries formed church-related networks beyond their area of service. In Louisville, several ministries discuss common concerns through the Association of Community Ministries and engage in joint fundraising through the Fund For Community Ministry. Thus, there is a kind of ecumenical movement going on between community ministries. Moreover, antipathy toward the ecumenical movement is barely noticeable in areas where community ministries organize themselves under the aegis of councils of churches while remaining independent from them. One finds community ministries staff members joining the National Association of Ecumenical Staff, using Ecumenical Networks resources, and showing interest in the National and World Councils of Churches.

We cannot tell whether the community ministry movement will converge with the ecumenical movement. But community ministry may yet provide a new and decisive connection between congregations, denominations, and ecumenical structures.

Here is a vision: If ecumenical denominational offices encourage greater functional unity of ministry at the local level, if the ecumenical movement comes to a wider doctrinal consensus and a more developed theoretical basis for unity, if the community ministry movement broadens its agenda to include working toward church unity as well as cooperative action, then very little will stand between cooperating congregations and more or less complete integration of local ministry.

The more dramatic set of contingencies has to do with the community ministry movement and whether it will establish mutually supportive relationships with ecumenical and denominational structures. As an uncertain factor, community ministry could pull congregations away from their denominations' priorities in social ministry, and they could make the conciliar structures even more irrelevant to local church life than they are now. They could either contribute or detract from a functional unity of ministry. Thus we have a volatile movement that might become a reactionary one, preserving the essentially competitive relationships among congregations, denominations, aspects of ministry, and types of ministry. This question of the future of community ministry deserves the consideration of denominational and ecumenical offices and of everyone who hopes for a vibrant and vital ecumenism for the sake of the world.

Practical Notes on the New Ecumenism

Within a community there may be pairs of congregations that enjoy a special relationship based on a history of cooperation or on cooperation between the respective denominations. Community ministry affirms and encourages these special ties. They add to the cohesiveness of a community ministry that, in turn, adds a dimension to the special relationship. Moreover, they tend to broaden the community ministry agenda to include "faith and order" concerns.

In regard to cooperative funding, any of the resources given to a community ministry by its member congregations and parishes presumably could be put to good use through denominational channels. Therefore, the only thing that prevents conflict between community ministry and the denomination is a willingness on the part of the denominations to promote ecumenism between congregations.

Where denominational commitment is shaky, it takes a special measure of independence for a parish to support community ministry. Although the reality is changing, community ministry has less claim upon congregational resources than does the denomination.

The relationship between community ministry and the denominations is complicated and requires much sensitivity on the part of both. In general, community ministries could not exist without the ecumenical best intentions of denominations. At least, life would be much harder without them. Yet the larger and more established community ministry becomes, the greater the potential for friction and the greater the testing of the denominations' commitment to ecumenical and cooperative ministry.

4   Starting and Developing a Community Ministry

Governance and Board Development

THE CONGREGATIONS who establish the ministry and whose volunteers, facilities, and money make it possible for the ministry to begin operations generally constitute the ministry's membership. Even in those cases where there is a broader membership base, there must be some effort to encourage congregational participation since it is the congregations that furnish the ministry with its mandate. Therefore, it is not unusual to find that only congregations are members and that only they are represented on the boards of directors.

On Long Island, at The Ministries, however, membership is open to any individual or organization who consents to the purposes of the ministry. Seats on the board are apportioned to congregational, denominational, and other institutional representation. A few seats are reserved for at-large representation by individuals. Nevertheless, congregational membership is almost always a key element in the governance of community ministry. The congregations position the ministry for service. Their membership legitimizes it as their extension in the community.

When a congregation becomes a member, it brings along at least four important constituencies: its members with their friends, relatives, and associates; its denomination and the relevant structures therein; its official board; and its pastoral staff.

The boards and the staffs of member congregations are especially important in the governance of community ministry.

The official board, regardless of whether it holds the ruling authority or merely advises the pastor, represents the character and direction of the congregation or parish as no other group does. Pastoral staff come and go, but the lay leadership core of a congregation tends to stay. Thus, when we use the term *congregation*, we mean primarily this group of leaders that at any given time most represents it. Thus in starting a community ministry, the key consideration is: Do we have a proposal that is acceptable to, endorsed by, or written with the participation of the official boards of the congregations of the neighborhood?

The pastor and his or her staff are probably the most influential factors in the decision of a congregation to join a community ministry. Moreover, they are instrumental in funding, interpretation, and program development. Depending on their perspective, they are part of both the generative core of the ministry and its clientele. That is to say, the ministry serves them through information, consultation, and program. It serves as a channel through which the larger community relates to the congregation.

How Pastors View Community Ministry

Some pastors have a tendency to view community ministry as a painless way of discharging their social ministry obligations. This "client" posture is much to be preferred over indifference! For one thing, such a pastor at least recognizes the importance and legitimacy of local social mission. For another, he or she might be counted upon to interpret the community ministry in the congregation. Finally, when pastors defer to the laity to represent them in the ministry, this option may be seen in a positive light so long as there is communication between lay representatives and pastors. The client posture may be a beginning place for the relationship between a pastor and a community ministry.

Those pastors who choose a more participatory stance, on the other hand, almost always become key leaders of the ministry. They have much to contribute in theological foundations, in group process, and in a sense of what is appropriate. They do not have to be social ministry firebrands to make a special contribution, because frequently, what might appear to be purely pastoral considerations lead to cutting-edge programs. Their participation should always be welcomed and cultivated. It should be remembered that pastors do not score points either among their peers or their congregations by participating in the community ministry. Chances are, such participation does not appear on their job description.

Contact between pastors and the executive director of a community ministry should not be limited to official meetings. The executive director should be in continual contact with pastors by telephone, written communications, and face-to-face meetings. It may be helpful to call an occasional meeting of pastoral staffs to ask for advice about crucial decisions that are before the board of directors, since any decision made by a board will die if pastors actively oppose it.

It is important for community ministries to encourage regular joint meetings of pastoral staffs without attempting to impose a pattern or agenda on the meetings. Depending on the interests of those who compose the group at any given time, the type of meeting could vary from year to year—from an informal breakfast with no agreed-upon agenda, to a formal lunch with a carefully planned program, to a self-designed course of study. It is in the best interests of community ministry to encourage such meetings and to listen carefully for clues as to the expectations, hopes, and assumptions of pastoral staffs.

Church Secretaries: Crucial Links

Church secretaries are key to the communications system of any community ministry. There will be regular contact between the community ministry office and the secretaries. Preferably, there will be personal contact between them and the executive director for the following reasons: Secretaries are important sources of referral; are frequently asked to explain what community ministry is all about; are often influential with the leadership of the congregation; are helpful in reserving church facilities or in locating volunteers with specific kinds of expertise; are good at providing communications resources such as directories, committee lists, schedules, bulletins, and newsletters; will give advice on how best to interpret the work of the ministry in the parish or congregation; and may be key persons in the life of the larger community as well.

Church secretaries are often an essential part of community ministry by virtue of their being on the front line in regard to requests for emergency assistance. A ministry does well to base its emergency assistance program on the cooperation of secretaries. It might sponsor a secretaries' lunch once every two years for the purpose of exchanging views and advice about emergency assistance and other subjects.

A Proposal Committee: The First Step Toward a Board

The original leadership group for any given community ministry might be called a proposal committee. This is the group that gathers initially to discuss the possibility of forming a community ministry in a particular neighborhood or area. The proposal committee would best include both poor people and those who work on behalf of the poor in the area, along with other interested people. It should involve those who feel directly the lack of certain services or supports, as well as those who are sensitive to the possibilities of an ecumenical, local, social ministry. The proposal committee should incorporate the advice of those who will be asked later to endorse and fund the proposal, the perspectives of human service professionals whose cooperation the community ministry will need, and the input of those who will be served. Thus the resulting proposal will be a product of the very community within which the ministry will operate. It will also be a product of the religious groups which will form the spinal cord of the organization.

The role of the proposal committee is not necessarily to produce a document that will be immediately acceptable. Rather, the committee will draw up a first draft after listening carefully to various sectors of the community. The proposal will include a long-term vision and a five-year projection with specific plans for funding, staffing, facilities, and program development. Good work on the part of the proposal committee is the best guarantee of getting smooth transitions between the talking, organizing, and operating stages.

Thus once a group decides to start a community ministry, it does not immediately start to organize. First, it is essential to have broad involvement in formulating the ministry—especially by all who have some stake in a local social ministry—and to have a wide spectrum of endorsements by congregations and other local institutions. These are necessary in order for the organization to establish its identity as a ministry that is part of the community. The authenticity of a community ministry may depend on not trying to organize too soon.

A Steering Committee: The Second Step

Once a proposal has gained a measure of acceptance, the proposal committee ceases to exist and a steering committee presides over the organizing/pilot-project stage. The steering committee represents the institutions willing to sponsor the start-up of a ministry. It possesses the resources and motivation to determine the nature of the first operations. In the case of The Ministries, a steering committee was organized before incorporation and the formation of a board. An executive director was hired to recruit the steering committee, which was then empowered by the participating congregations. For that period the community ministry functioned under the corporate identity of one of the sponsoring institutions: the Presbytery of Long Island.

Highlands Community Ministries incorporated at the beginning of the organizing/pilot-project stage, and for the first twelve to eighteen months of operation, a group of pastors functioned as an interim board of directors or steering committee.

There is no set sequence for incorporating, forming a board of directors, hiring an executive director, and doing pilot programming. No matter what the sequence, governance will be provided by a transitional interim group or steering committee.

A Board of Directors

In community ministry a board of directors is not a mere sounding board for the staff, doing nothing more than giving advice or lending their names to the organization. Nor is it primarily a group of fund-raisers. (Nevertheless, the board does have responsibility for fund-raising and may want to establish a separate structure for the purpose.)

Neither is the board like those of certain business corporations that hire staff to run the organization and that intervene only to evaluate and replace the staff if their work does not come up to expectations. Such boards relate exclusively to the executive, holding him or her responsible for the work of the staff. This professional model contradicts the basic understanding of community ministry as a ministry of the laity. To assign the work of the ministry and its direction exclusively to professionals and their staffs is an avoidance of the responsibilities of church membership.

On the contrary, the ministry's board of directors is a participatory and involved body, usually composed from the rank and file of congregations, that makes all the major decisions regarding policy, program, budget, and staffing. The board plays an active role in assessing need, evaluating program and staff, and interpreting and supporting the ministry in the churches and in the community. The members of the board are all regarded as community ministers in their own right who may be involved in some aspect of the daily operations of the ministry and who are expected to keep themselves informed about it.

Goal Setting and Planning

The rise of community ministry roughly corresponds to the rise of various organizational planning processes that emphasize the setting of goals and objectives, strategies and tactics, as a means of achieving identity, cohesion, direction, accountability, and productivity. The survival of many community ministries over the years has depended upon use of these processes.

As experiments themselves, community ministries are generally open to innovative approaches in fields that bear upon their development. In fact, some community ministries have attempted to pioneer a field of organizational planning. (For example, through its training programs, the Wall Street Ministry of the early 1970s in New York City was a major force in the so-called Organizational Development Movement.)

Also, as experiments, community ministries need methods for objective self-evaluation. This attention to process, as time-consuming as it may be, has borne the fruit of self-respect and effectiveness in dealing with agencies and institutions in the community at large.

Board Member Orientation

The advantages of well-planned and executed board member orientation programs are well known. In community ministry these sessions serve as training in ecumenical and social ministry. Often, new board members will have little concrete experience in organized ministry and few conceptual/theological foundations. However, they will have valuable competencies and genuine (if vague) commitments to ecumenical and social ministry. Thus they require a primer in the concept and practice of community ministry. The following outline is currently in use at St. MAM:

1. Fundamentals of Social Ministry—biblical and theological foundations of, types of, ministry as the prerogative and responsibility of all baptized members.

2. Principles of Ecumenical Cooperation—biblical and theological basis, practical problems associated with the ecumenical movement, interfaith cooperation, unity for the sake of the world.

3. The Community Ministry Movement—biblical and theological rationale for, concept of, genesis and history of, taking responsibility for building community where we are.

4. Our Particular Ministry—our community and the emphases of our ministry, our history, constitution, policies, program, staff, budget, facilities, the meaning of our presence in this community.

5. Board Members' Responsibilities and Opportunities—governance, church and community relations, interpretation, fundraising, committees, meetings, assignment to specific tasks.

Staffing Community Ministries

A consensus is emerging that a newly formed community ministry ought to have as a goal the hiring of a full-time paid executive director. The engagement of an executive director sends a clear message to the community that the churches are serious about caring for the community. This position is really an investment in the community on behalf of the churches.

In most cases we have found that the degree to which the churches commit themselves to that goal is the degree to which they are prepared to work together within the framework of community ministry. In our local Association of Community Ministries the main requirement for membership is that the financial support of the constituent churches amounts to the provision of at least a full-time executive director.

This requirement also addresses considerations of the effectiveness of social ministry. A salaried position supported by the churches goes a long way toward assuring the independence of the ministry. It is much safer to accept governmental or private funds with this financial backbone in place.

Certainly a problem in recent years is that community ministries are being started with the encouragement of local or state governments to assist in the delivery of public assistance programs or to supplement such programs. These ministries find it doubly difficult to achieve a lasting commitment from congregations and parishes, and sooner or later, the dependence on governmental funds for the continuance of operations is experienced as unduly restrictive if not repressive.

Occasionally one finds a congregation that hires a "community minister" for its staff. These churches evidently recognize the importance of the points that we have just made, but the impact of church staff positions does not compare with that of an executive director of a community ministry. The church staffer is almost always perceived as representing the interests of his or her own congregation. There are rare instances, however, where the congregation has such a tried-and-true record of disinterested service in the community that such is not the case.

There are instances in which congregations have assigned

part of a staff member's time to the community ministry. Frequently, this option—as an alternative to hiring an executive director—leads to a truncated ministry.

Calling an Executive Director

Persons have been hired to the post of executive director from almost every imaginable background. They have tended to be either ordained ministers or social workers, however. In the former case they will usually have experience in social ministry, including community organization, social action, or social service. In the latter case, they generally will have ties to a faith community and experience in working with church-related organizations. The social worker is in an excellent position to model the lay ministry aspect; the ordained minister may be more adept at interpreting the work to the faith communities.

The unique needs of each community have produced about as many approaches to hiring as there are ministries. The one generalization that may be ventured is that they tend to be eclectic in their hiring! Boards often require a master's degree or its equivalent, but they might not specify a field of study or they might be generous in their interpretation of "equivalent." There are executive directors who do not have a graduate degree and some who do not have an undergraduate degree.

There are few resources to guide boards through the hiring process. The recently formed national Interfaith Community Ministry Network eventually may be of assistance. Theological seminaries and schools of social work are becoming more attuned to the professional requirements of community ministry. The Ecumenical Networks group of the National Council of Churches has for some time distributed guidelines for the hiring of ecumenical executives, and a related body, the National Association of Ecumenical Staff, has an active committee on professional standards whose work promises to be helpful to community ministry.

The Role of Executive Director

The executive director should be regarded primarily as a program developer. Most executive directors, even in the largest community ministries, are necessarily deeply involved in program development and implementation as well as in general administration. Thus, it is a serious interpretative mistake to charge the salary of the executive director to "administration" in the annual budget. Executive directors will be found behind their desks less than half the time. They will be in the community, in the churches, at the program sites; they will be out developing resources, contacts, and cooperative relationships. They will be found listening to the community in many ways.

Executive directors must be willing to embrace the role of fund-raiser from the very beginning of their tenure. There have been numerous attempts to evade this role, but to no avail! The only professional fund-raiser to which the ministry is likely to have access during the first ten years of its existence is its executive director.

An executive director who is also a professional minister may be expected to carry some denominational responsibilities, and these ties may be valuable for the ministry. In fact, denominational support can be a crucial factor in its success. Thus there is something to be said for negotiating the terms of a new executive director in cooperation with his or her denomination. It is well to remember that the denomination to which the executive director belongs may take a special interest in the ministry.

The Support Staff

The secretarial, bookkeeping, and financial management functions will have to be provided for from the very beginning, perhaps through a combination of paid and volunteer time, perhaps through hiring someone who can combine more than one of these roles in one job.

Community ministry operates in a glass house. It has literally hundreds of bosses in pastors, church staffs, members of church boards, public officials, and the people to be served. It simply cannot afford to be shoddy in communications, record keeping, or financial procedures or in fulfilling legal requirements. Within the first eighteen months of existence the following needs will arise: to have a system of regular communication to the various constituencies; to incorporate; to obtain federal tax-exempt status; to obtain insurance; to arrange space-use agreements; to have a budget development process; to have a financial policy and procedures statement, monthly financial reports, an outside review or audit, a bond for those who handle money, and the capacity to capture the actual financial situation on any given day; and a system for recording, acknowledging, and following up contributions or potential contributions.

Thus the newly formed ministry will have to fill the following roles rapidly and in this order: executive director/program developer, secretary/communicator, and bookkeeper/financial adviser, either through paid or volunteer staff.

Program Staff

It is not unusual for a community ministry to consider engaging program staff within two years of its birth simply because otherwise the executive director is not free to perform the full scope of his or her tasks, including the development of programs and projects.

Certain conditions must be met, however, before the program staff is hired. A framework of support must be set up that includes a clearly stated endorsement of the program by the board, the assurance of a six-month to one-year budget, and the recruitment of a volunteer program committee that is responsible to the board and that has the capacity to oversee the program and the program director.

Program Directors

A program director is accountable to the executive director and to the board through a program committee. He or she can be charged with interpreting the work of the entire ministry in the community and, through specific means of cooperation and communication, furthering the work of the entire ministry.

The combination of a dedicated, functioning program committee and a devoted, competent program director may obscure the need of integrating this program into the ministry as a whole. Understand at the outset that a program director will have a critical impact on both the community and the ministry and that the interests of the two may seem to clash at times from the perspective of the program. Good working relations between program directors and executive directors require regular and open communication.

Ideally, executive directors and boards will be clear about where they stand on the issue of centralization when they hire a program director and recruit a program committee. For example, if they would like a program to be self-supporting within a specified period, they should not be surprised if that program takes a rather independent stance. At the other end of the spectrum, a centralized model requires a central office with certain capacities for servicing the programs. A resourceful program director, not finding the needed administrative resources right at hand, will find ways of moving ahead at the expense, if need be, of closer ties to the central office.

These tensions are all but inevitable in the development of community ministry program because there will always be a gap between the needs of the community and the joint response of the churches, and it is, after all, only right and proper that the claims of a community—felt most acutely through the programs—will result in difficult challenges and choices for the board of directors.

Program Committees

A program committee supports a program director in important ways by furnishing a leadership core dedicated to the goals of the program, a constituency within the larger framework of the ministry, a source of constructive criticism when it is needed, and expertise in the field. It functions in much the same way as a board of directors and, ideally, has the same kinds of legal, financial, personnel, public relations, and fundraising expertise, as well as expertise in a particular field. Without a functioning program committee, we run the risk of producing an isolated and demoralized staff, a program that is more expressive of the needs of staff than of the community, and the absence of the local participation and lay involvement that energizes the community ministry movement.

The most problematic aspect of staffing a program is that the program may take on a life of its own that detracts from the ministry as a whole. Therefore, the program director and committee ought to have a vision of how their program fits into and contributes to the larger picture.

Other Staffing Considerations

In most community ministries, staff does not determine policy and program, and the strong chief-executive-officer model does not apply. The *staff and executive director* take their orders from an active and participatory *board of directors*. In implementation, as well, staff must be sensitive to the people in the pews who are always present through the various levels of volunteer participation. Staff members—as well as everyone else—influence the organization in the give-and-take of relating to the local community over the long term.

There is relatively little turnover of executive and program staff in the field of community ministry. It appears that this circumscription of powers and participatory style has had its salutary effect.

Equal Employment Opportunity and Affirmative Action (EEO and AA) belong together because they represent two important aspects of nondiscriminatory hiring and personnel practices. EEO generally refers to the requirements of the law. Meeting these requirements may be a condition for receiving government funds, and more may be required than just a statement disavowing discrimination. The applicant may be asked to submit an EEO plan that covers hiring, promotion, and grievance procedures. Less is required, however, of the smaller organizations, and enforcement of these laws has slackened in recent years. Recent federal administration has actually sought to narrow their applicability.

Affirmative Action, on the other hand, refers to that which an organization undertakes to do above and beyond what is required by law. AA embraces goals and standards that the organization sets for itself and reviews at regular intervals. AA means that a community ministry goes out of its way to assure that nondiscriminatory personnel policies are followed for women, racial-ethnic persons, older persons, and persons with disabilities.

Affirmative Action is especially important for community ministries because the ministries experience little pressure from EEO laws and may not feel at all constrained by the EEO standards of denominational or larger ecumenical entities. Moreover, being as local as they are, their mission areas may be relatively homogeneous. These are all reasons for an intentional and vigorous affirmative action policy.

Who in the organization is responsible for EEO and AA? Only the executive director is in a position to emphasize the intention of the organization and to monitor personnel practices from a position of authority. It is the responsibility of the board of directors to see that the executive director performs this function by receiving annual reports on the status of Affirmative Action and by including a consideration of it in their annual evaluation of the executive director.

Collegiality in both style and form is an ideal arrangement for community ministry. For many years The Ministries, one of the largest and oldest of community ministries, was led by codirectors—a priest and a minister. The codirectors embodied the ecumenical aspect of community ministry. The priest was a child of the area, having been raised and educated there. He was a member of the county human rights commission when his bishop assigned him to the community ministry. The minister, who also had a background in social ministry, had been called to the area by his denomination to conduct a one-year mission exploration. Thus the two personified not just the ecumenical dimension but the social, experimental, and local dimensions as well.

The codirectorship stimulated a general spirit of participation and proved to be a model of leadership for program development. Their youth ministry opted for codirectors—one leading a residential program for status offenders and the other leading a drop-in counseling service in a regional shopping center. The two, a woman and a man, found that their relationship to the youth constituency was enhanced by the form of leadership that had been chosen.

This collegial form of leadership, when it is practicable, has the potential to symbolize the participatory nature of community ministry and to multiply the benefits of professional leadership. The coexecutive directors became outspoken advocates of collegial leadership patterns in their respective faith communities.

It may not be necessary to produce a personnel practices manual for a ministry that has one or two employees, but it is necessary to have the *terms of employment* in written form and to let the relationship be governed by definite policies that are a matter of record. These documents form the basis for a manual that should include provision for annual job performance evaluations and salary reviews, processes for airing grievances and resolving differences, encouragement of training and continuing education, stipulation of holidays and vacation time, and a description of health and retirement benefits and pay scales.

The ministry should be clear about what it expects from its employees and about its own obligations. Most employees of community ministry probably work for less remuneration than could be earned elsewhere, and many actually volunteer additional unpaid hours. It is all too easy to take such dedication for granted and drift into a pattern that is exploitative of employees. Vigilance is required!

Personnel policies could well be evaluated and updated every two or three years with the advice and consultation of employees. Whereas the staff implements these policies, the personnel committee of the board monitors them.

To some, *staff development* means the articulation and deployment of staff positions in a growing organization. To others, it means the opportunities for growth that an organization affords its staff. In community ministries these two considerations go hand in hand.

A staff knows when the workload is exceeding its capacity or when specific functions are required that no staff member can fulfill. Thus the decision to establish a new staff position, whether full-time, part-time or volunteer might well be the result of discussions among and with the staff.

The professional growth of employees depends to no little extent on the degree of support they experience during a typical working day and on the quality of interchange between employees during the day. New staff positions can be described in such a way as to enhance these growth factors for current employees. For example, if the new position involves a new program or project, then the discussions will focus on how the new program will interact with current programs in ways that will add to their effectiveness.

Any new position should be regarded as accessible by current staff as an opportunity for their professional growth. One of the most elaborate community ministries in the United States, the East End Cooperative Ministries of Pittsburgh, is directed by Judith Marker, a former teacher, who had started out in the organization as a part-time coordinator of volunteers. She was full-time director of the children and youth program when the executive director resigned. The board asked her to assume the position of interim executive director and proceeded to conduct a wide-ranging search. After a time, they realized that she was the one they had been looking for all along to fill the position.

The Ministries of Long Island appointed their youth services program director, Clarence Jones, to the position of executive director even though it meant a reorientation of his vocational goals to embrace the larger context.

St. MAM, which has a large after-school day-care program, promoted one of its caregivers, Janet Hennessey, to the position of program director although she had no formal education beyond high school. She and the ministry agreed that she would pursue certain educational goals. After six years, this program director had earned a college degree in her field and added several credits toward a master's degree. While achieving these goals, her program tripled in size, and she was invited to serve as a consultant to several governmental and private child-care agencies.

Staff development as described above occurs with gratifying frequency in community ministry, which is to say that the growth of the organizations is coinciding with the professional growth of their staffs. This characteristic of daily work in community ministry is a concrete benefit of the juxtaposition of social ministry and the concept of "parish." Since operations are focused on and contained within a clearly demarcated area or locality that is relatively small, there is the opportunity—indeed, the necessity—to put the needs and wants of the people before the aggrandizement of either the staff or the organization, benefiting everyone concerned in the long run.

Funding Community Ministries

That which sets community ministry apart from other non-profit or ecumenical organizations is its integral relationship with constituent churches. Translated into financial terms, the member churches make an annual pledge to the ministry just as their members make annual pledges to the churches. These pledges are the financial backbone of the ministry. A community ministry must inspire member congregations in the same way that congregations inspire their members to commit to an annual pledge that will cover the essential costs of operation.

With time, other kinds of funding might exceed that of the congregations. However, congregations almost always remain the most important funding source; their funds guarantee the survival and independence of the ministry and legitimize its presence in the community. Like the work of community ministry in general, fund-raising is congregation-based and participatory.

The Basis for Congregational Financial Participation

A community ministry does not come to congregations as an *outside* organization. It comes to them as a constituent part of each congregation. This claim, however, is valid only insofar as the congregations themselves recognize the unique relationship—a fact that underlines the importance of interpreting the work of the ministry in the congregations, showing how the program of the ministry derives from pastoral concern for that very community, showing why the program cannot succeed without congregational participation on several levels, being visible and present in the congregations in various ways, and demonstrating an integrity of ministry in which the educational, evangelical, liturgical, and communal aspects are wedded to the social and ecumenical ones.

Determining Amounts of Congregational Support

There is no formula for determining the amount of monetary support that a congregation might contribute. Statistically, congregations pledge from one to twelve dollars per year per adult member in addition to contributions that do not appear in the budget (from special offerings, church school classes, and other groups or individuals). There is no standard amount, but when a congregation decides on its contribution, the amount should say to anyone that looks at the church's budget that the community ministry is an integral and important part of the church's mission. Only the members of that church themselves really know how this guideline gets translated into dollars and cents. Never try to evaluate the annual pledge of a congregation on the basis of comparisons with other congregations or parishes.

Not all congregations will be connected to denominations that have a long-standing commitment to the ecumenical movement, and their participation is much harder won. Churches of the "ecumenical" denominations may be expected to shoulder a proportionately greater part of the burden.

Nor is it easy to compute the real total financial support of a congregation. One must take into account the use of facilities, the involvement of church staff, and assistance in obtaining funds from other sources. One must also take into consideration other social and ecumenical ministry commitments of the congregations. Community ministry should not seek financial support at the expense of these other commitments. Congregations, like individuals, often have unique financial circumstances that are not fully understood outside the immediate family.

If the parish is supporting a school (as is the case with most Catholic parishes), that school is considered a form of community ministry. It is next to impossible to compare the finances of a

Catholic parish, in which seventy-five percent of the budget supports a school, with that of a Protestant parish of the same size.

The Long Road to Financial Security

Some ministries have raised millions of dollars in the community at large. Some now have considerable assets consisting of real estate, motor vehicles, up-to-date office equipment, and restricted and unrestricted funds of various kinds. Yet there are very few for whom congregational support is not the most important source, even fewer for whom at least part of the program is not in constant financial jeopardy, and none who can afford to delegate fund-raising to a committee or expert. Thus the board as a whole is well advised to take seriously its responsibility for financial stability.

Let those who are just starting a community ministry note that almost no community ministry achieves any degree of financial security until it has passed the fifteen-year milestone. Until then, a ministry may well be satisfied in the knowledge that it has enough commitments to cover six months of operations at a time. Furthermore—claims to the contrary notwithstanding—a track record of less than fifteen years, even a very successful record, does not lend itself well to major public fund-raising efforts.

Ministries can certainly benefit from professional fund-raisers who are willing to volunteer advice, but these considerations should not be allowed to obscure the central importance of congregational support. It is always in that light that we must consider the major categories of financial support for community ministry: congregations, government and United Way, corporations, individuals, special events, endowments, and other funds. Doing so will also require discussions on documenting need, grant writing, and fund-raising policy.

Documenting the Need

Community ministry assists congregations in understanding the community by documenting and describing its needs. This same documentation may be used in presentations to foundations, government, and other potential funding sources.

Material descriptive of the community may be found in the reports of parish pastoral care teams. The problems and needs of parishioners will provide clues to the state of affairs in the larger community. Other methods of needs assessment will help to document the need.

Whenever a budget is submitted it should be accompanied by a rationale that contains evidence of continuing need for the program. These rationales, though submitted in the first place to the board of directors, will become a part of the fund-raising documentation. Ministries that find they are the object of study by research institutions and individual students can claim and use the results of this research in documenting the need for funding.

Annual evaluations will serve not only to assess the performance of staff and the ministry as a whole but may also serve to pinpoint the places where additional funding is crucial. Evaluation serves to image an organization that is not afraid to be self-critical. Evaluations may originate with the board of directors, the staff, individual congregations, denominations, the people who are served by the programs, private and governmental funding sources, or educational institutions that are conducting research or that have field education on the scene. Any of these may be asked to initiate an evaluative process, and each would have a uniquely helpful perspective from the standpoint of fund-raising.

Finally, community ministries have many opportunities to sponsor conferences, consultations, and other types of meetings that have positive ramifications for fund-raising purposes because they generate information that may be used in documenting the need, they enhance the status of the sponsoring organization as a responder to community needs, and they stimulate networks of cooperation that help to assure the implementation of program.

Grant Writing

Next to nourishing its ties to congregations, the most important fund-raising activity of community ministry is grant writing. Grant requests are submitted to foundations, businesses, government agencies, and denominational offices. A typical community ministry may submit dozens of proposals within a two- to three-year period. These requests are based on master proposals that are tailored to suit potential funders.

The proposal to establish the ministry is its first grant request. Addressed to a broad constituency, it will produce funds during the first several years of the ministry's existence. It should document the needs to which the ministry will respond and make a convincing argument that the community would benefit from such a ministry. It should, in fact, be a joint product of several sectors of the community, illustrating a spirit of cooperation in the writing itself, and it should assure the reader of plans for board development, needs assessment, evaluation, and longer-term funding.

At a minimum, any grant request must state precisely the purpose for which funds are being sought, describe and document the need, and convince the grantor that the organization has the capacity to implement the objectives of the grant request.

Grant writing is a skill that takes time and patience to identify potential funders, to write the grant and compile supporting documentation, and to follow through in communication with the grantor, even if the request is denied on the first try.

Therefore, the staff and board members should possess as much grant writing experience as possible. They should be encouraged to get specialized training. Nothing substitutes, however, for working side-by-side with an experienced grant writer, beginning with the first telephone call and including the writing, submission, and follow-up of the request. One might be told how to write a grant, but what makes an indelible impression is observing someone craft a grant request while explaining at each juncture why they say this or that.

Numerous resources are available to fledgling grant writers. Grantors may be willing to clarify their expectations and priorities, and they are sometimes willing to lend assistance with the process of submission. Complete information on local foundations usually can be found in the public library. Among the members of congregations may be those who have expertise in grant writing and the ability to identify potential donors.

A word of caution and a plea for foresight: Grants are not permanent! Usually, the larger the grant, the less permanent it is. It would be rare for a grant of more than twenty thousand dollars to be renewed more than twice or for a grant of ten thousand dollars to be renewed more than four times. It could be argued that for the typical community ministry, several small grants is to be preferred over one or two large ones.

Government and United Way

There are ministries that do not apply to either the government or United Way as a matter of principle. They might not want to be bound by the restrictions of the United Way or they may not wish to be identified with the philanthropic establishment in their locality. Some rule out government sources as well in order to guard their independence and/or to avoid the appearance of violating the principle of separation of church and state.

Yet community ministry has some unique advantages in regard to these two funders. Local government or the United Way may fund a community ministry program over an indefinite period. When funds for human services are on the increase, the ministries are good bets for experimentation and implementation of new programs, and they are avenues of community outreach. Moreover, when funds are short, ministries may present themselves as a means of economizing because of their access to volunteers and their low staff and facility costs.

The character of both the United Way and local government funding varies a great deal from place to place. Some would be more controlling and restrictive than others. In some communities local government and the United Way, through interlocking directorates, exercise a hegemony over the delivery of social services that is felt by grass roots organizations as oppressive.

A ministry might decide on a case-by-case basis whether to submit proposals to a United Way or government agency depending, for example, on whether there is congruence in priorities between the community ministry and the funder. The best guarantee of a ministry's independence—vis-à-vis the government or

United Way—is its own clearly stated priorities and the support it receives from member churches that sustain operations when grants are not forthcoming.

Special Events

Special events are both more and less effective than other means of raising funds. On the plus side, they can be major social events for the community and its churches, and they are opportunities for education and interpretation. A bowlathon will promote good will among bowlers; a game booth in an annual community festival will increase visibility; a horse show will make fund-raising contacts.

On the other hand, special events require many hours of planning and preparation as well as volunteers with consummate organizational skills. Unless such a core of workers can be produced, it is better not to try the special event since an unsuccessful one will have a demoralizing effect and use up valuable staff time. These events generally become a more effective part of a community ministry's funding after two to four years' operations. They may serve as a bridge to individual donors. Occasionally a ministry will raise upwards of 10 percent of the annual budget through special events, but more often the figure is 5 percent or lower.

Individual Solicitation

Almost every instance in which ministries engage in individual solicitation began as a last-ditch survival effort after several years of resistance. Once established, however, individual giving becomes a mainstay of community ministry support. The Ministries has an elaborate, staffed system that includes direct mailing. United Crescent Hill Ministries in Louisville has had several years of successful individual solicitations based on personal contact.

There are several reasons this method is the last to be used in community ministry. It runs the risk of undermining the crucial relationship with member congregations. At first, ministries do not have access to the large corps of volunteer workers that is required to run a successful campaign. Individual solicitation is predicated upon a certain level of visibility in the community, an understanding of the ministry's concept and purpose, widespread and meaningful contacts with individuals—all of which may take several years of operation. Thus, during their first years, community ministries rely almost entirely upon sources other than individuals.

Nevertheless, ministries may want to consider using this method at times other than when under the threat of imminent closing. Fund-raising experts seem to be nearly unanimous in saying that one should not assume that donors will not want to contribute directly if they already contribute indirectly (through a congregation). Moreover, the solicitation of individuals is an opportunity to educate persons about the ministry and to involve them to a greater degree.

Finally, when a ministry has been operating for five years or more, it is almost certainly the case that there are persons who are truly grateful for its presence and who are willing to help to assure its future through a personal contribution.

Fees

Fees are a part of the funding structure of those ministries that are engaged in the delivery of direct services. They may account for more than 50 percent of a ministry's income, particularly if it administers large child-care or family counseling programs.

Fees have a deeper significance for community ministry than first meets the eye. They make the ministry a participant in the local economy. The ministry renders itself accountable to the community at large by its promise of delivering a service that is actually worth more than the fee. The ministry demonstrates its financial integrity in the setting, collecting, and recording of fees.

For those who cannot afford to pay the fees at the set level, the ministry can offer either a sliding scale or "scholarships" on a case-by-case basis. Those who have little or no income may be asked for a nominal amount, partial payment at some unspecified time in the future, or for a contribution of time in lieu of cash—if any of these seem appropriate; that is, if it contributes to a person's self-respect and to his or her participation in the ministry.

There is a principle of reciprocity and participation even when there is no fee as such. Recipients of emergency financial assistance may be asked for information that will help in the search for structural solutions; or they may be given opportunities to participate in representations to various branches of government on behalf of the poor.

Endowments, Restricted Funds, and Other Funding

Until recently, this was a category of support beyond the scope or imagination of the mostly fledgling ministries. Lately, however, many ministries twenty years old or older are interested in establishing funds, the principal of which remains intact for the long term or until it may be used for a designated purpose. The oldest community ministries have discovered that they have potential donors, some of whom have expressed an unsolicited interest in their ministry. Financial advisers are saying that the realities of the 1990s are making it important for even small nonprofits to have capital and endowment assets. Rank and file volunteers, who have invested as much as twenty to thirty years' service, want to do what they can to assure the future of the ministry.

A Fund for Community Ministry:
One Approach to Corporate Donors

All corporations and businesses within the mission area and all that are represented among the volunteers of the ministry should be solicited at regular intervals. In cities or counties with more than one community ministry, it is worthwhile to consider coordinating the solicitation. Corporations often are not interested in contributing to an organization that is identified with just one part of a metropolitan area, but ministries can band together for the purpose of submitting joint proposals.

In Louisville, thirteen community ministries have formed the Fund for Community Ministries, with guidelines for membership, solicitations, and distribution of grants received. The fund has raised an average of one hundred thousand dollars annually during its first three years—not enough to represent a breakthrough for the larger ministries, but large enough to have a positive impact on the budgets of the smaller ones.

The fund has benefited the ministries in unforeseen ways. For example, a group of young professionals that was raising funds for the needy during the holiday season decided to use the fund to distribute the amounts that were raised. The fund has also been a means for redistributing resources for the benefit of the younger or poorer ministries, for encouraging the formation of new ministries, and for raising the general level of cooperation between the ministries.

Fund-Raising Policy

The financing of community ministry is a subject that is much debated, and if the issue is not to be divisive, a fund-raising policy should be placed on the record and revised every few years. On the basis of policy, decisions may be made in response to the myriad fund-raising ideas that will be brought to the staff and board. If the ministry wants to rule out certain broad categories of funding, a policy statement serves the purpose. Under the exigencies of financial hardship, many schemes and proposals will be put forward, some of which—if accepted—will alienate portions of the constituency or prove to be unworkable. A fund-raising policy serves as a basis for rational reflection on the subject and protects staff and board from being pushed into hasty decisions.

A Problem of Success

The Problem of Fragmentation

The problem of fragmentation in a developing community ministry contains several aspects. Among the most important are the needs of a single-function program division under a generalist board of directors, the special funding requirements and opportunities of developing programs, and the double task of program directors both to advance their program and to effect intra-agency cooperation. The following are illustrations of each of these aspects of the problem.

A Program Goes Independent (1)

A community ministry organizes an equal opportunity housing services program as one of its first efforts. After several years, the program incorporates as an independent entity. On the board of directors there is some disappointment and resentment not only because of the decision of the program to go independent, but because—in the period between its inception and incorporation—the program seemed to follow its own interests and contributed little to the success of the ministry as a whole. Other members of the board argue that the spin-off was a good idea and should be a model for future programs of the ministry. Still other members of the board express relief that the program went on its own because they do not really understand the housing field.

A Program Goes Independent (2)

In its first year a community ministry starts a senior citizen program. After a year of special events and projects, word comes of the availability of substantial governmental funds for a community-based program. The program committee determines that it wants to become independent, apply for the government funds, and hire its own executive director. The budget and area of service expands to several times that of the parent organization. Some on the board of directors resent the departure of the program and are anxious because the newly independent organization requests funding from the same sources that the ministry depends on, including its member congregations. Others on the board say that it is just as well that they do not have to be involved in the administration of substantial government funds. They argue that the uncertainties of funding and the demands on staff would have been serious drawbacks to the continuing development of the ministry.

A Program Goes Under Other Auspices

A ministry endorses a new program and a new conceptual approach to the problem of drug and alcohol abuse. The program grows rapidly, doubling its budget in each of the first four years of operation. Its fund-raising capacity far outstrips that of the more longstanding programs of the ministry. The program director and the program committee decide that it would be in the best interests of the program to become independent. Members of the board express dissatisfaction with the program director and the program committee, saying that the latter did not appreciate the role that the parent organization played in the success of the program and that the program was too unstable to become independent. Other directors say that the program would be better off on its own. The decision is made that the program not become independent. The program director and members of the program committee resign. The program is eventually taken over by a new chemical dependency department of a local hospital with the approval—and the set conditions—of the board.

How Fragmentation Develops

These stories illustrate how program development may lead to fragmentation as programs acquire a life of their own and grow rapidly within a comparatively weak parent organization.

The program committee and its staff acquire expertise in a field where the board may have very little. The tendency of a successful program is to function as a corporation with a single purpose within the community ministry. Once functioning as such, it is a small step to actual independence.

Underlying these illustrations is the fact that, often, funding sources are not interested in the community ministry as such but only in the particular program and in objectives related to that field. Moreover, in the case of most grants, the few funds that are available for overhead would go to the administration of the particular program rather than to the community ministry. Programs discover funding sources and methods of raising funds that are particularly appropriate to the programs themselves. As a result, programs have a tendency to develop an entirely separate fund-raising apparatus alongside that of the parent organization.

Related to all of the above are the roles of the executive director of the agency and the program director. The executive director gives the program director high marks as the program expands and attracts more funds, clients, and constituents. But the tendency of the program director—under the pressures of an expanding program—may be to give only token attention to building up the community ministry as a whole.

Community ministry boards generally do not have the expertise to give direct oversight to particular programs. Thus they generally form program committees that are really commissions delegated to oversee the program, including staffing and the administration of its budget. Although the program committees report to the board, they have considerable freedom in everyday operations and in shaping the direction of the program. The program committee may co-opt expertise that is not available on the board of directors.

To some extent, fragmentation is a problem inherent in community ministry, one to which each ministry will find its own solution. How each one resolves the problem will, to a large extent, determine its unique character.

Conclusion

More than any other factor, it is the vital institution we call the congregation that has produced the community ministry movement. The multifaceted and variegated world of the congregation is at the root of the unique aspects of community ministry. The many constituencies of the congregation are constituencies as well of community ministry and are the keys to its future.

Community ministry gives several congregations a joint territorial parish in which to carry out social ministry. It reintroduces the congregation to its neighboring peoples and institutions, but it also helps to interpret them within their wider contexts and their claims upon grass roots ecumenical and social ministry. Community ministry brings all the many dimensions of the local community home to the congregation.

Community ministry is a joint expression of care for the totality of a specific mission area on behalf of several congregations in that area. Pastoral staffs and committees have proven to be good sensors of need, and the community ministry is the repository of a wealth of information about the community. The priorities of a community ministry are shaped by this information in the context of pastoral care. Thus the effectiveness of community ministry depends upon the willingness of congregations to make resources available to programs as extensions of their own ministry.

The potential contribution of community ministry to social justice and ecumenical relations is unlimited to some but problematic to others. To what extent does the local provide clues for understanding the global? Does community ministry function as an escape, as a means to reduce ecumenical and social responsibility to the strictly local? Or does it bring these responsibilities home to the religious community in a new and effective way? The current era is a proving ground for community ministry in respect to these questions.

Community ministry is having an impact on ecumenical/interfaith and social ministry. Congregations find more relevance in community ministry than in more traditional ecumenical structures based on denominationalism and the prerogatives of the clergy, but denominations will play an important role in the future of community ministry.

Community ministry belongs to its congregations and to the people of the community, of which the congregations are a part. This is the reality that determines everything from board composition and governance processes to staffing patterns and job descriptions. Its executive director or codirector develops programs on behalf of the churches and the community. Its operations are subject to broad local scrutiny.

Community ministry programs maintain a dual loyalty: to the people for whom they were called into existence to serve, and to the churches of which the programs are an extension of ministry. This tension is built into community ministry and represents a challenge from the standpoint of organizational development. Program directors, in particular, feel this tension in the form of pressing claims from both the population they serve and the church constituencies (though they often overlap).

The financial viability of community ministry depends upon its being "owned" by congregations and the local community. Community ministries earn this status by faithfully listening to, documenting, and interpreting the community to the community itself and its congregations. All other efforts to raise funds (for example, through grant writing) are supported by this central interpretive task.

When community ministries cooperate in fund-raising, they possess an extraordinary potential vis-à-vis government (as a delivery system), corporations and foundations (as grass roots, yet metropolitan by virtue of cooperation), and the general public (as representing the building and maintaining of community on the basis of residence). Moreover, by cooperating in fund-raising they model the spirit of unity that they seek to encourage among member congregations and parishes.

In time, the whole range of fund-raising instrumentalities will become available to community ministries, including direct mail, individual solicitation, and the establishment of endowments and other funds, restricted and unrestricted. Furthermore, ministries may establish fee-for-service programs with the advantage of a trusting predisposition on the part of large segments of the community.

In a word, community ministry is well positioned in the social, political, economic, and religious scene to sustain a growing movement of national proportions in the neighborhoods, small towns, and rural counties of America. We are now engaged in fashioning a new form of ecumenical and social ministry, one that takes its bearings from clusters of congregations, each of which is unique. These share a local culture that is itself unique, and they choose to care for their community together. It is hardly possible to predict what the final character of the movement will be, but it is entirely safe to say that it is now a major opportunity for the church.

Notes

1. Nathan van der Werf, "The Fabric of Ecumenism," *Association of Council Secretaries Journal*, June 1971.

2. Stan Esterle, Interview at Highlands Community Ministries, Louisville, Ky., spring 1989.

3. Ibid.

4. Barbara Solomon, unpublished address, "Empowering Our Communities," presented at Consultation on Community Ministries, Louisville, Ky., April 1988.

5. Ibid.

6. Dieter Hessel, *Social Ministry* (Philadelphia: Westminster Press, 1982), 188; and in the revised edition (Louisville, Ky.: Westminster/John Knox Press, 1992), 191.

7. Joe Holland and Peter Henriot, S.J., *Social Analysis: Linking Faith and Justice* (Maryknoll, N.Y.: Orbis Books, 1983, xx, 1–30). Relying on Paulo Freire's *The Pedagogy of the Oppressed* and Juan Luis Segundo's *The Liberation of Theology*, Holland develops the notion of a "pastoral circle" that brings social analysis into pastoral care. In this process, social analysis precedes pastoral planning. It "serves as a tool that permits us to grasp the reality with which we are dealing."

8. Esterle, Interview at Highlands Community Ministries, Louisville, Ky., spring 1989.

9. "Ecumenical movement" is a term that refers roughly to the period from 1900 to the present, during which time there was a grand rapprochement of several Protestant communions. Their coming together to form the World Council of Churches in Amsterdam in 1945 was preceded by the formation of several arenas of cooperation, including the International Missionary Council, the Life and Work movement, the Faith and Order movement, and resistance to fascism during World War II. They supported the formation of "councils of churches" at every level (metropolitan, provincial or state, national, regional, and international), all except the most local (neighborhood and village).

These councils were not formally related within a superstructure. The one thing they had in common was that they were creatures of agreements between the same denominations. The denominations used the movement to implement an agenda that involved a marriage between "faith and order" (considerations of doctrinal and structural unity) and "life and work" (collaborations in specific projects, programs, and social reform). While there was always a genuine openness and desire to address theological and social concerns together as Christians, the denominations also used the movement as a foil for the articulation of their separate identities and for the protection of their interests within the arena of ecumenical politics. The marriage of faith and order and life and work was not extended to relations between congregations because, insofar as the denominations used the ecumenical movement as a foil, it was not in their interest to encourage ecumenical relations at the most local level possible.

Walter M. Abbott, S.J., has said that the Decree on Ecumenicism of Vatican Council II "marks the full entry of the Roman Catholic Church into the ecumenical movement." *The Documents of Vatican II*, ed. Walter M. Abbott (New York: Guild Press, 1966), 339.

10. I affirm the insights of James Hopewell in his *Congregation*, ed. Barbara Wheeler (Philadelphia: Fortress Press, 1987).

Wheeler writes about his essay in the foreword: "The two apparently ordinary congregations [where Hopewell had spent a sabbatical leave as a participant/observer] have extraordinarily rich, dramatic, textures. Though located only a block apart in a small town, each drawing members from the same economic stratum of the town's population, the two churches were strikingly different from each other in ways their Baptist and Methodist affiliations did not explain. Each, [Hopewell] concluded, had a distinct culture, as unique and rich as those of the religious communities he had served and studied as a missionary in West Africa early in his career (vii)."

11. Wade Clark Roof and William McKinney, *American Mainline Religion* (New Brunswick, N.J.: Rutgers University Press, 1987), 44.

12. William Thomas, comments made as a panelist at the National Consultation on Community Ministries, Pittsburgh, Oct. 25, 1991. Used by permission.

13. See records of the Kentuckiana Interfaith Community (successor organization of Louisville Council of Churches).

14. This estimate is based on the author's acquaintance with thirteen community ministries of the Louisville metropolitan area and community ministries associated with the Interfaith Community Ministries Network.

15. See reports of the Association of Community Ministries, Louisville, Ky. In the 1990 restructuring of the National Council of Churches, the equivalent of one and one-half staff persons were was assigned to Ecumenical Networks, the successor to the Commission on Regional and Local Ecumenism, which had been assigned the equivalent of two staff.

Bibliography

The Congregation and Social Ministry

George Webber and Letty Russell began to write from the context of the East Harlem Protestant Parish, which I would call the first of the modern-day community ministries. Those first works, *The Congregation in Mission* (Nashville: Abingdon Press, 1964) and *Christian Education in Mission* (Philadelphia: Westminster Press, 1967), are excellent background material for our movement. Their later works reflect their earlier experience and are relevant to ecumenical and local community ministry, especially as regards the participatory aspect. I refer in particular to Russell's *Human Liberation in a Feminist Perspective* (Philadelphia: Westminster Press, 1974); *The Future of Partnership* (Philadelphia: Westminster Press, 1979); and *Growth in Partnership* (Philadelphia: Westminster Press, 1981); and Webber's *Today's Church* (Nashville: Abingdon Press, 1979). From the recommended booklist of the latter work I would underline Gibson Winter's *The New Creation as Metropolis* (New York: Macmillan Co., 1963) and Elizabeth O'Connor's *Call to Commitment* (New York: Harper & Row, 1963).

The one book that I would call a "must" on this subject—because of its challenge to congregations to do ministry holistically and because community ministry is one possible response to that challenge—is Dieter Hessel's *Social Ministry*, rev. ed. (Philadelphia: Westminster Press, 1992). Representing the congregational studies field and indicative of the possible interface between it and community ministry is James Hopewell's *Congregation* (Philadelphia: Fortress Press, 1987).

Heralds of the Community Ministries Movement

Works began to appear in the 1960s that contained radical critiques of local church structures and that stimulated many of us to entertain visions of local and ecumenical social ministry. These included Steve Rose's *The Grass Roots Church* (New York: Holt, Rinehart & Winston, 1966) and his edited volume *Who's Killing the Church?* (Chicago: Chicago Missionary Society, 1966); Colin Williams' *Where in the World* (New York: National Council of Churches, 1963); Gibson Winter's *The Suburban Captivity of the Churches* (Garden City, N.Y.: Doubleday & Co., 1961); and Gayraud Wilmore's *The Secular Relevance of the Church* (Philadelphia: Westminster Press, 1962).

Related Movements

Latin American liberation theologies, black and feminist theologies, and the ministry of the laity movement have all influenced and contributed to the growth of community ministry insofar as they have advocated greater respect for the local in the formulation of ministry. The following works in particular come to mind: James Cone, *Black Theology and Black Power* (New York: Seabury Press, 1969), and *God of the Oppressed* (New York: Seabury Press, 1975); Paulo Freire, *Pedagogy of the Oppressed* (New York: Seabury Press, 1970); Gustavo Gutiérrez, *A Theology of Liberation* (Maryknoll, N.Y.: Orbis Books, 1973); Constance Parvey, ed., *The Community of Women and Men in the Church* (Philadelphia: Fortress Press, 1983); George Peck and George S. Hoffman, eds., *The Laity in Ministry* (Valley Forge, Pa.: Judson Press, 1984); Juan Luis Segundo, *Liberation of Theology* (Maryknoll, N.Y.: Orbis Books, 1976); Sharon D. Welch, *Communities of Resistance and Solidarity* (Maryknoll, N.Y.: Orbis Books, 1985), and *A Feminist Ethic of Risk* (Minneapolis: Fortress Press, 1990); Gayraud Wilmore, *Black Religion and Black Radicalism* (Maryknoll, N.Y.: Orbis Books, 1983).

The Community Ministries Movement

This burgeoning movement has produced little literature. Two books have appeared recently that treat some aspects of community ministry. Carl Dudley's *Basic Steps Toward Community Ministry* (Washington, D.C.: Alban Institute, 1991) is a summary of Lilly Endowment funded research on how congregations do social ministry in their communities. Like an earlier book by Dorothy Bloom, *Church Doors Open Outward: A Practical Guide to Beginning Community Ministry* (Valley Forge, Pa.: Judson Press, 1987), there is almost no mention of the ecumenical dimension that is so crucial to the movement. A further drawback to Bloom's book is that she speaks from a strictly Southern Baptist perspective.

William Cate has written *The One Church in This Place* (Seattle: Institute for Ecumenical Studies of the Northwest Theological Union, 1991). Cate is a grandparent of the community ministries movement. While director of the Portland, Oregon, Council of Churches in the early 1970s, he encouraged the development of community ministries there. His book *Ecumenical Scandal on Main Street* (New York: Seabury Press, 1969) was written in that context. The thesis of his new book is that the real ecumenical movement is happening at the local level.

Also see my "Community Ministries: The Establishment of Ecumenical Local Mission in North American Church Life," *Journal of Ecumenical Studies* 22:1 (Winter 1985): 121–127; and my "Community Ministries: The Wild Card in Ecumenical Relations and Social Ministry," *Journal of Ecumenical Studies* 25:4 (Fall 1988): 592–598.

There are two foreign-language books that deal more specifically with community ministry as we have defined it here than anything that has appeared in English. One, in Dutch, is titled *Kerk en buurt* ("Church and neighborhood: Theological and sociological commentary on the relation between church and neighborhood in four old urban districts"), by K. A. Schippers and J. B. G. Jonkers (Kampen: J. H. Kok, 1989). The other, available in French, is titled *Vers de nouveaux oecumenismes* ("Toward new ecumenisms: The contemporary paradoxes of ecumenism:

Attempts at unity and quests for identity"), edited by Jean-Paul
Willaime (Centre de Sociologie du Protestantisme de Strasbourg, 1989).

One finds an interesting and candid, if incomplete, international overview in *Local Ecumenism*, edited by André Birmele
(Geneva: World Council of Churches, 1984), the final report of a
four-year study project suggested by the Sixth Assembly of the
Lutheran World Federation in Dar-es-Salaam in 1977 and car-
ried out by the Institute for Ecumenical Research in Strasbourg.

For a brief overview of Great Britain's Local Ecumenical Projects (LEPs) see the journal *One in Christ* 25:2 (1989): 158–160.
Since they are "authorized" community ministries, the local
community is far less determinative of their development than
in the United States, but the specifically ecumenical aspect is
more apparent.